Twayne's United States Authors Series

EDITOR OF THIS VOLUME

Kenneth Eble

University of Utah

Albert Halper

TUSAS 352

Albert Halper

Photo by Lorna H

ALBERT HALPER

By John E. Hart

Albion College

TWAYNE PUBLISHERS

A DIVISION OF G. K. HALL & CO. BOSTON

Published in 1980 by Twayne Publishers,
A Division of G. K. Hall & Co.
All Rights Reserved

Printed on permanent/durable acid-free paper and bound
in the United States of America

First Printing

Frontispiece photo of Albert Halper © by Lorna Halper

Library of Congress Cataloging in Publication Data

Hart, John Edward, 1917–
Albert Halper.

(Twayne's United States authors series;
TUSAS 352)
Bibliography: p. 145–50
Includes index.
1.   Halper, Albert, 1904–
—Criticism and interpretation.   I.   Title.
PS3515.A3867Z69   813'.5'4   79–21080
ISBN 0-8057-7291-X

Once Again
to
Mary Helen
and to
Oliver Twist

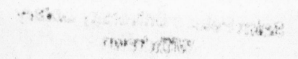

Contents

About the Author

John E. Hart received a doctorate degree from Syracuse University in 1954. He has been writing since the early 1940s. Some of his poems found their way into little magazines, and he was for some ten years a member of Alan Swallow's Experimental Writers Group. He has published scholarly articles about Stephen Crane, Nathaniel Hawthorne, William Dean Howells, Mark Twain, F. Scott Fitzgerald, Ernest Poole, and a study of the Felix Fay trilogy by Floyd Dell. He has been teaching literature and composition at Albion College since 1954.

Preface

Albert Halper published his first story in 1929. During the next decade, reviewers and critics seldom failed to mention his name as one of the bright new story tellers whose knowledge of urban life and social conditions had helped to establish new directions in American writing. With the end of the 1930's and America's entrance into World War II, public interest in social reform had already given way to new concerns for self-preservation and individual prosperity. Although Halper continued to write and publish during the postwar period, critics and readers alike have all but ignored his contributions to the literary world of both past and present.

With renewed interest in the 1930's and a reexamination of that crucial and fascinating era by literary critics and historians, references to Halper seldom do more than link his early work with the new proletarian writing, which was never his concern, or with the political left, with which he was only vaguely sympathetic. Consideration of his writings has hardly gone beyond brief mention of *Union Square* or *The Foundry*; his work seldom appears in college anthologies. His novels have never been made into movies or television specials. He has been not so much misinterpreted as neglected and forgotten.

The initial study of a writer—and of a forgotten writer at that—must be something of a rescue operation. At this writing his books are generally not obtainable in modern editions; only a third of his shorter pieces were ever available in book form. The originals of these publications remain scattered in magazines where they were first published; many of them were never available to a large reading public and are now difficult to find, even in large libraries. Halper's manuscripts themselves are not readily available; publishers have apparently, in some cases, already destroyed letters and memoranda that might have added understanding to the work of a writer who has always been a very private person, fairly spurning personal publicity, interviews, the lecture platform, and all public appearances.

Still, throughout his works Halper has already talked freely about his experiences, about his ideas and his writing. The few letters that have made up my own correspondence with him have been incisive, rewarding, courteous, and helpful. Some of his correspondence with Viking Press, which Marshall Best has made available to me, reveals the artist at work, the man who pursued his craft with diligence and care. Surely a critic must respect and even honor a writer who answers questions with brevity and candor, but who preserves the integrity of his personal life with friendly refusal. "You will find everything you need to know about me in my writings," he advised. ". . . I have no comments concerning my theories of writing . . ."; "an author either has talent or he hasn't, and his work is judged accordingly." Surely Halper's own writing is ample evidence of an author's talent, of his energy and insight, of his independent spirit, his ability to write spirited and forceful prose.

This study is based, then, almost wholly on Halper's writings, and since he wrote about his life repeatedly, sometimes using similar material in stories and novels, the evidence tends toward repetition. Although his range is narrow, he has written a meticulously accurate account of what it was like to live and work in the mechanized jungle of our cities during the 1930's. He explores the life of city streets, the working conditions of factories and stores, and he writes with the authority of the worker who has known those streets and worked at the very jobs he describes. His memories of personal experiences and impressions of people and places, especially during the era of the Depression, provide a vivid picture of the American scene.

Although most of Halper's writing is fictionalized autobiography, this study aims to be a critical analysis of his work, and not a biography. My aim has been to reveal the scope and nature of his work, to chart the course of his development, to note his successes and failures as a writer and as a social critic. The book is organized chronologically. Chapter 1 describes his early life. Chapter 2 deals with his life in New York as he established himself as a writer. The next four chapters analyze some of the short stories and the five novels that appeared from 1933 to 1943. The remaining chapters examine his various publications after World War II and comment on his contribution to American letters. Much of my own evaluation lies not in final judgment on a writer whose work needs further exploration, but in the analytical descriptions of the writings themselves. Since Halper invariably wrote against a background of current social conditions, any study of his writing is also partly the study of an historical era. That era may not soon repeat itself: as a Cambridge graduate told

Preface

C. Day Lewis, the decade of the 1930's "seems to be the last time that anyone believed in anything."

Grateful acknowledgement is made to Albert Halper for permission to quote from his writings, for his answers to my many questions, for providing a bibliography of his works, and for reading the manuscript and checking it for facts and information. In addition, I sincerely want to thank the following: Dr. Sylvia Bowman, who suggested the project; Marshall Best, editor at Viking Press, who generously made some of Halper's letters available; Dr. Edward N. MacConomy, Chief Bibliographer for the Library of Congress, who guided my search in the beginning; Lotus Snow, Elizabeth Hosmer, and Albert Peters for reading the manuscript and commenting upon it; Bruce Keeling, for the many discussions on writing and writers; Michael Noble, for sharing his knowledge of Chicago; Albion College for a Faculty Fellowship Award for the summer of 1972; the library staff at Albion College for their assistance in solving all kinds of reference problems; MHH, for her enthusiasm and constant help along the way.

JOHN E. HART

Albion College, Michigan

Chronology

1904   Born in Chicago, Illinois, "around Lake Street and Ashland Avenue," August 3, to Isaac and Rebecca (Alpert) Halper, Lithuanian Jewish immigrants. Next to the youngest in a family of three older brothers, one older sister, one younger brother.

1912   Grew up on Chicago's West Side; attended Tilden grammar school; worked in his father's grocery store.

1917   Entered John Marshall High School, 3250 West Adams Street, in September.

1918   Worked as errand boy in John T. Shayne & Company, a fur and haberdashery store, State Street side of the Palmer House.

1921   Graduated from high school, June 22. Composed popular songs; none was published. Worked as order-picker at Philipsborn Company, a mail-order house, 511-515 South Paulina Street.

1922   In the autumn, began work at The Chicago Electrotype Company, an electrotype foundry, located in the R. R. Donnelley Building at 731 Plymouth Court. Remained there four years.

1923   Enrolled in Chicago-Kent College of Law in September, but withdrew in less than two weeks.

1924–   Attended Northwestern University Evening Divisions,
1927   School of Commerce, from September 9, 1924, to June 6, 1926. Worked at various jobs for brief periods: as promotional salesman for R. J. Reynolds Tobacco Company; as salesman in 1926 for H. R. Gibbs and Company, a wholesale beauty parlor supply house on Wabash Avenue; as clerk in a jewelry store: as machine-operator in a factory making loose-leaf binders.

1927   *Purple Pudding* (poems), privately published in May. Enrolled in Citizens Military Training Corps in July; served at Fort Sheridan, Illinois. Mother died August 7, 1927. Began work as postal sorter on the night shift at the Central Post

Office on Jackson Boulevard and Clark Street, where he worked for fourteen months.

1928   Left Post Office in Autumn and went to New York to write. Met Elliot Cohen, editor of *Menorah Journal*.

1929   "Whites Writing up the Blacks," first publication in *Dial* magazine, January. Returned to Chicago and did research in a law office. In September, returned to New York, which became his permanent home. Maxim Lieber became his literary agent. Friendships with Kenneth Fearing, Louis Adamic, Charles Reznikoff, Tess Slesinger. Wrote *Good-bye, Again*, his first unpublished novel.

1930   Spent summer at Yaddo Artist's Colony, Saratoga Springs, New York, where he completed *Windy City Blues*, his second unpublished novel. Worked on a third unpublished novel.

1931   During the summer, worked as a waiter and skit-writer at a camp for adults at Warrensburg, New York.

1932   Finished writing *Union Square*; publication delayed when Literary Guild book club chose it for its March, 1933, selection.

1933   *Union Square*, March.

1934   *On the Shore* (short stories), February. *The Foundry*, published in September. Received Guggenheim Fellowship in creative writing in late summer. Went to London, worked on a novel, and met Edward and Constance Garnett. To the Soviet Union in April, 1935. Returned to New York in early summer; refused an offer from *New Masses* to go on a lecture tour.

1935   Father died in August.

1937   *The Chute*, October.

1940   *Sons of the Fathers*, October.

1942   Married Pauline Friedman, January 6. *The Little People*, October. A son, Thomas, born on December 1.

1943   *Only an Inch from Glory*, October.

1948   Visited by FBI in August for information about an alleged connection with a left-wing underground organization to which Max Lieber belonged.

1952   *This Is Chicago* (anthology), October.

1953   *The Golden Watch* (related short stories), March.

1954   *My Aunt Daisy* in collaboration with Joseph Schrank, a play produced by the Theater Guild at the Westport Country

Playhouse, Westport, Connecticut, in August. Starred Jo Van Fleet and Leslie Nielsen.

1955   *Top Man*, a play produced by Albert Lewis and I. B. Josselow at the Shubert Theater, New Haven, Connecticut, in November. Cast included Polly Bergen, Ralph Meeker, and Lee Remick. Closed in Philadelphia, Pennsylvania, in December.

1956   *Atlantic Avenue*, a Dell First Edition Original Novel. Marriage to Pauline Friedman ended in divorce. Urged by Leonard Ehrlich, joined staff of City College of New York as instructor in creative writing; remained one semester. Married Lorna Blaine Howard, an artist, December 28.

1966   *The Fourth Horseman of Miami Beach*, October.

1967   *The Chicago Crime Book* (an anthology), November.

1970   *Good-bye, Union Square*, November.

1979   Lives in upstate New York.

CHAPTER 1

Early Life to Remember

CHICAGO, said Albert Halper, "was never a bad town for writers. . . . It was always a good place for a writer to be born in, or to grow up in. And after a Chicago writer reaches adulthood it doesn't matter where he lives, in New York, Paris, or Rome. The silver cord is never cut, he never really gets away." [1] Halper left Chicago in 1929 for the second and last time, and although he lived in New York and traveled to London and to Russia, he remained a Chicago writer. When he finally settled in New York never to live in Chicago again, he returned to his memories of the city, to his recollection of little events and personal happenings that his responsive and sensitive mind had witnessed and stored away. Out of such remembrances the young writer gave shape and pattern to his experiences and to the lives of the simple and honest people that he had known in a place where survival meant eternal awareness of the harsh and bitter assaults on their lives and living meant personal struggle and endurance. The city that he had known as a youth and young man and the hallmarks that he ascribed to it—its forthrightness, its inner honesty, its individualism, even its lack of nicety of style—were to be his hallmarks as well.

Halper remembered Chicago as never dull and seldom tranquil, one of the newest and liveliest cities on earth, but also one of the most complex, with, as he writes, "the shifting stance and unpredictability of a heavyweight wrestler. . . ." The visitor may well be jolted with "its tempo, its rawness, its beauty" as if with a "stiff electric charge." Always attractive to writers and artists, Chicago nurtures their talents and then lets "them drift away." "More than any other city in the world," Halper writes, Chicago "sets out food for her children and her stepchildren, then turns her face away." [2] This indifference shows up dramatically in the writers—Theodore Dreiser, Floyd Dell, Carl Sandburg, Sherwood Anderson, Willa Cather remained for a while and left. By the end of the 1920's and early '30's, a new generation of writers that included James T. Farrell, Meyer Levin, and Albert Halper had begun to explore new experiences and a new environment. City-bred and city-nurtured, they tended, as Dale Kramer has pointed out, "to portray the ethnic groups from which they had emerged." [3] If they had inherited a literary tradition, they had also inherited a city that continued to thrive on beef and lard, on soap and shoes, on guilt and graft, a city of big money and large ideals, of immigrants and ethnic groups, a city still as generous and as cruel to the artist as it had always been. These writers also moved on.

Because Halper's early life is inextricably bound up with Chicago and with his family and relatives who lived and worked there, these factors have become the vital stuff of his fictional world and of his writing. Coming from a Jewish-Lithuanian heritage and growing up in a completely urban background, Halper not only inherited the brash, brawling, hustling aspects of the city with its sights and noises and smells and slangy rawness, but also a city that had a "feeling of deep inadequacy, a sensitivity to fine things, an aching for the sun." [4] Readers of his stories and novels will confront the contradictions of the city and of his life over and over as he probes beneath the facade into the stuff of memory with findings that are varied and intricate and inexhaustible and somehow more real than facts.

I   *Life on Chicago's West Side*

When Halper's father and mother arrived in Chicago in the early 1890's, immigrants from Slavic nations were very much in the minority. Even by 1920 Lithuanians made up less than twenty thousand of the city's total population, a mere trickle from the "rushing stream" which had begun in the late 1880's and had accelerated around 1891 and again in 1901. Isaac and Rebecca (Alpert) Halper had grown up in Lithuania, in a small village near Memel on the Baltic Sea. Halper's father had come from a large family that had already begun to go their separate ways by the time he came to America. One brother had gone to New Zealand; another to British South Africa. Two brothers, including Halper's father, had come to the United States and finally to Chicago. Arriving just before the great Columbian Exposition in 1893, Isaac Halper and his wife had sought a new life in the new world, bringing with them their few belongings, their old-world ways, and firmly held Jewish traditions, arriving, like so many other immigrants, "over the Baltimore & Ohio, pulling in at the old Polk street depot." [5] They settled on Chicago's West Side and with a little money opened a small grocery store. During that first ten years, times were difficult; the whole country was recovering from the economic problems of the early '90's. The family grew; three sons and a daughter arrived before Albert was born, "around Lake Street and Ashland Avenue," on August 3, 1904.

Chicago's West Side was a dingy, dreary place, with a variety of shabby stores and dwellings and a mixture of ethnic groups. Ashland Avenue, once the "Bonton Street" of the West Side, had boasted such estates as that of Carter H. Harrison, Sr., onetime mayor and boss of Chicago, a place where fawns and peacocks roamed the lawns. The area had fallen into decay; the estate had become Union Park; Carter Harrison's statue and the memorial to the Haymarket Riot recalled the West Side's colorful and paradoxical past. Now the area sprawled into the "gray land mass" that was industrial Chicago. As Halper recalls, it contained "grim miles of factories laced with railroad sidings servicing printing plants, clothing shops, juke-box assembly lines, the biggest mail-order houses, machine-tool manufacturers and a hundred other 'hard goods' lines." [6] "Here," he wrote elsewhere, "is the modern city, the vast industrial jungle, the web of viaducts, and the blight. Here is labor's home." [7] The West Side contained "colonies of Swedes, Germans, Jews, Czechs, Sicilians and Poles . . . who man this city's production machinery." [8] A smaller, but duller and bleaker Negro belt than that found on the South Side struggled along West Lake Street "under the black girders of the El." [9] Even the young carried identifying marks of West Side residency: "As a youthful West Sider," Halper recalls, "I used to travel to ballrooms all over the city. No sooner had I paired off with a girl than my style of dancing was recognized, sometimes archly. 'You dance different. I bet you're from the West side.' " [10] Bleak, gray, depressing, the West Side was also home.

Making a living for a growing family was no easy matter. Hours in the grocery store were always long. Halper's father opened the store around four-thirty in the morning to catch the early trade and remained open until late in the evening for the stray shoppers, who usually made only small purchases. Like most neighborhood stores, he carried a little of everything, catering to a local clientele and to the transient laborers who had nearby jobs. "Of all the foods he sold," Halper recalled, "I remember best the hams, the boiled hams. I can see the ham ends now, small and fatty, resting in the icebox: my old man's weekly problem, his eternal struggle with profit and loss. If he didn't sell the end of a boiled ham he lost out—for embedded in it was the sixty or seventy cents profit he made on the entire ham." [11]

Always there were problems. The hot weather might come suddenly and spoil the few slabs of fresh meat in the "dinky ice-box." Customers on credit sometimes skipped out and never paid. The new chain-stores were apt to move in and ruin business for the small merchant.

When conditions got too bad, the family moved to a new location, often living upstairs above the store. As Halper recalls, they were forever moving westward, from 1520 Lake Street across from Union Park to Taylor Street, Oakley Avenue, Fulton Street; finally to 426 North Kedzie Avenue, where they remained for eleven years, their longest stay in any one place. The stores were invariably small. In 1914, the stock, housed in a building perhaps twenty feet long and fifteen feet wide, was, Halper remembers, worth around $500.

Operating the store became a family affair. The older boys helped out, just as Albert and a younger brother did, taking turns waiting on customers, going to market, and delivering groceries. Young Albert took charge of the book department that the Chicago Public Library had installed in hundreds of small grocery and candy stores throughout the city. Books ordered one day could be picked up the next and, for such a service, the store owner received a cent a copy. In his spare time Halper began to read, mostly "wild Westerns," which he seldom finished. Nonetheless, they inspired him, and under their influence he took to scribbling before he was ten years old. He knew little of the classics; he had never heard of a poet.[12]

The store became more than a livelihood for Halper's family. Along with regular attendence at grammar school and high school and services at the nearby synagogue, working in the store became a social and economic training ground for the young writer. He learned about new ways of living and new values from his older brothers, already employed by a downtown clothing firm. As traveling sales-men, they rode the trains into the growing towns and villages of Illinois and Iowa, returning home with new clothes and sometimes gifts, joking and laughing and telling about their experiences. He learned about the customers in his father's store, the penny-pinchers, the down and out, the whiners and complainers. On delivery runs that took him into the homes and lives of long-time neighbors and newcomers to the city, he heard their stories, their complaints, their hopes and fears. On the streets, he witnessed racial violence and hatred as white punks attacked blacks or young Irishmen attacked young Jews. Sometimes he helped his father pick up supplies in other parts of Chicago, not always as grimy and forbidding as the gray West Side.

Alone in the store when his father went home for meals or when business was slack, he had time to dream, time to listen to the sounds of the city, to catch the chug of a nearby locomotive, the wail of a train's whistle, the roll of moving freight cars on the old Northwestern railroad. Not far away the Lake Street Elevated roared and crashed along. The smell of the stockyards drifted over the city. The streets were a cry and wail of discordant sounds. "I was born," he wrote later, "in a raw slangy city, in a raw slangy neighborhood." [13]

Neighborhood street life offered few easy lessons. He watched the young hoodlums zipping by in their flashy roadsters; or a farm boy, new to the city, being accosted by city punks; and young girls at the soda fountain, already wise to the ways of young men. He remembered the long hot nights of the West Side. Young men sauntered along the crowded streets, idle and easy in their ways, cat-calling to young girls, jostling each other along the curb, acting a bit cocky, indulging in big talk. If young men seemed "free and easy," Halper knew from experience that they were also "young fellows with hard rows to hoe." Some of them wanted more. ". . . underneath it all," he recalls, "was a vague dull ache, and we couldn't put our fingers on the nerves that made it." [14]

Seasonal change implied a shift of pace, a new feeling. In autumn when the wind blew hard and leaves fell, the smoke rolled in from the factories; in spring the dust whirled along the street as the days grew warm; "husky fellers and broken geezers" lined the curbs East of Halstead Street, where the cheap employment agencies did their business. Election day brought bloody brawls at the polls; sometimes young men, even one-time buddies, turned into successful gangsters. The young loafed at "The Corner" nearby Madison Avenue and Paulina Street, a few blocks from Lake and Ashland, "without knowing that it was the crime center of America." Much later he learned that "a certain saloon there became the mecca of cons arriving from prisons from all parts of the country." As he said, "All I was aware of was that it was a bleak neighborhood containing many saloons and the American Theater, a ten-cent movie house that I patronized every Saturday matinee." [15] He liked music; he liked to dance. He visited "all the ballrooms of the city, lured by the new name' bands." "We were all conscious of jazz," he remembered. By 1916 the South Side had begun sending out its new rocking, tumultuous jazz sounds. Louis Armstrong was already fast becoming legend. [16] When he was fourteen, he worked after school as errand boy for John T. Shayne & Company, a fancy fur and haberdashery establishment, then located in the old (the third) Palmer House on State Street and today still doing business on Michigan Avenue.

In September, 1920, he entered his senior year at John Marshall High School on West Adams Street and was graduated in June, 1921. He was only sixteen years old. As with his older brothers, his future lay in finding employment and working his way up through the ranks. A job as order-picker in a mail-order house was hardly an auspicious beginning.

The Philipsborn Company on South Paulina Street catered to rural areas of Southern and Western States, stocking mostly cheaply made items of clothing and household necessities. The workers were young and inexperienced; most of them had obtained working papers when they were fourteen and had already dropped out of school. The hours were long; the noise deafening. Some of the "pickers" wore roller skates to speed their work. They wheeled along the aisles, reading the letters and filling the orders with often the shoddiest kind of merchandise—"cheap work shirts, rubber collars, corduroy pants, fedora hats"—which the firm had picked up at auctions or bought from jobbers at a low price. After the orders were picked, as Halper recalls, they were "sent down into the giant chute leading to the assembly tables six floors below." There the items "were checked, wrapped and weighed for shipping." [17] The workers were hurried along by a system of bells that signaled with noisy regularity. The only high school graduate among the order-pickers, Halper earned thirteen dollars a week.

The job offered little satisfaction, but he dared not give it up. For a while he toyed seriously with the idea of becoming a song writer. He had never taken music lessons, but he could find chords on his sister's upright piano and bang out a few tunes. He had a flare for popular songs. He recalls coming home from a long day in the mail-order house, eating supper, and then trying out a few tunes to an unappreciative family, who thought the playing more noise than music. In "A Song Writer in the Family," not published until 1944 and only semiautobiographical, the narrator describes his brief career as a song writer. A couple of lines from "I Miss You, Corinne" are the only record of his endeavors. His forty-third composition, he writes, was not "that tinkling Zez Confrey stuff like 'Kitten on the Keys,' but the real McCoy from off Madison Street, the new Chicago style." [18] Or as Halper himself recalls, some small-time orchestra leaders "in hard-boiled roadhouses just beyond the city limits of Chicago" tried out a few numbers, but none of them ever saw publication or stampeded listeners into great applause. [19]

After more than a year with Philipsborn, he left the mail-order house in the autumn of 1922 for a better job as shipping clerk and plate stamper at the Chicago Electrotype Company, located in the R. R. Donnelley Building at 731 Plymouth Court. The job was demanding, but fairly easy. An electrotype consisted of a copper or nickel-plated duplicate of a copper etching or wooden engraving; it was used to illustrate all kinds of publications. Halper's job was to check the cuts according to scale, determine the price, make out the bill, and direct the errand boys in making deliveries to near-by printing houses. The job brought him in contact with both workers and bosses. He listened to their stories and arguments; he knew their quirks and frustrations. He saw what happened when a "new labor-saving machine" threatened a man's job or a lonely "finisher" wanted to "rent a room in the apartment of some wealthy widow." Sometimes, he went to their Saturday night dances, attended their weddings, joined them on the "company's annual picnics held on the prairie west of Chicago." He learned of their personal lives, their moods and temperaments, their fights and brawls, their joys and laughter. Critic and observer, he remained one of them, always the worker earning a living, absorbing the experience at hand, filing it away for future use.

Halper remained four years at the foundry, but he was still restless, still living at home, still dissatisfied with himself. He sought new directions. On September 12, 1923, he enrolled in Chicago-Kent College of Law, but withdrew on September 24, after less than two weeks. From September 9, 1924, to June 6, 1926, he attended Northwestern University Evening Divisions, School of Commerce, studying courses in writing, speech, psychology, newspaper reporting. He read constantly in Mark Twain, James Joyce, Knut Hamsun, Sherwood Anderson, Theodore Dreiser, the new writers F. Scott Fitzgerald and Ernest Hemingway. On "long wintry Sunday afternoons," he visited the Chicago Art Institute; he was "torn between the wonderful collections of the Italian primitives and the French impressionists." [20] He could afford only gallery seats in the theater, but visits to the Blackstone and the Garrick introduced him to a lifelong interest in the theater.

He still liked music. After working all day in the foundry, he recalls going home for a hasty dinner and rushing off to a dance at the Trianon or Dreamland, where everybody was trying new dance steps. He listened to the music of King Oliver, Charlie Straight, Bix Beiderbecke, Art Kahn, Paul Ash, Wayne King, and Paul Whiteman. Once he saw a "toddle" wedding, where the minister and the bride and groom all "toddled" during the ceremony. Chicago had a new name,

that "toddling town." Once on his way home he saw a fleet of beer
trucks tooling down Van Buren Street, followed by a black car and
four hard-faced men riding inside. It was as close as he ever came to
seeing Chicago's gangland at war. He had been writing a little, jotting
down impressions, making notes. For a while he even tried his hand
at poetry.

Halper published his first book in 1927, a small volume of poetry,
entitled *Purple Pudding*. He had dedicated the poems to his mother
and had them printed at a small shop across the street from the
foundry where he worked. The book's epigraph had supplied the
title: "Of Dreams and uneasy slumber—/ The result of PURPLE
PUDDING." [21] Of the hundred copies printed, only a few remain;
fifteen or twenty found their way into libraries and to friends and
relatives; later Halper destroyed the rest of the copies himself.

He recalls the volume with embarrassment. The thirty-eight
poems, most of them less than a page in length, are clearly those of a
beginner, but they show a concern for subject material that he will
develop later in the novels and stories. He writes on the "revolving
doors of an office building," on Municipal Pier, about Michigan
Avenue. "Love" uses the metaphor of a "little girl/ Dancing on a
sunny street in April." In "The Doubter," the speaker prefers death
rather than giving up being a doubter. In "We Who Wait," the "I" has
"schooled myself to wait," has "tusseled" with self and "risen the
master," but of what, he does not know. In "Do Not Follow," the
speaker's destination "is a million miles further" than the stars. The
poems reveal a sensitivity to seasonal changes in the city, a concern
for social conditions, the need for knowing self, the loneliness of man.
Using both rhyme and free verse forms, he shows none of the verbal
brashness that later becomes an identifying mark. *Purple Pudding*
neither merited nor received any notice; it shows little evidence of a
writer's talent.

Aimless and dissatisfied, Halper took other jobs. For a while he
worked as a "junior advance man for the R. J. Reynolds Tobacco
Company, trying to promote a . . . chewing tobacco plug called
Apple Sun Cured, to the Negro trade on the South Side." [22] When he
returned for re-orders, he was thrown out. He worked as a machine
operator in a factory making loose-leaf binders; clerked in a jewelry
store. In 1926 he became a floor salesman for H. R. Gibbs & Co, a
wholesale beauty parlor supply house on Wabash Avenue, but after a
year, he tired of the racy clientele and quit. A variety of jobs had only
left him more dissatisfied and had done little toward establishing a

direction to his life. In the summer of 1927, he enrolled in the Citizens Military Training Corps and spent the summer at Fort Sheridan, Illinois. With the death of his mother in early August, he returned to Chicago. As he said later in commenting on this period of his life, "Finally, I figured that what I needed was some sort of personal crisis so that I could find out where I was heading for. (This statement, on the face of it, sounds like heavy thunder in light opera, but at that time it was serious business to me.)" [23] Then in the late summer (1927), he took a job with the Chicago Post Office, where he worked for well over a year.

Becoming a postal clerk had involved a number of steps. The applicant first passed the civil service examinations for substitute post-office clerks. Before being sworn in, he had also passed a physical examination, appeared before the civil service board, and submitted to questioning. Having passed these hurdles successfully, he must then wait for an opening. Halper was assigned to the mailing division of Chicago's Central Post Office at Jackson Boulevard and Clark Street as a mail sorter on the night shift. His number was 437. As a postal substitute, but regular civil service employee, he was obliged to undergo a rigorous course of training, most of which had to be learned on the clerk's own time.

The business of sorting and throwing mail was fairly complicated. Each sub was given a certain state to learn. That state became his "scheme"—learning a scheme meant memorizing every town in that state, the county and township to which each town belonged, the days on which the trains did and did not stop at the town, and where necessary, the various ways of rerouting the mail. New clerks were carefully watched; each was given a certain amount of mail to throw in an hour; his pace was checked by a supervisor. If a clerk fell behind, he was quickly warned.

Nor was the work easy. Sorting the mail and slinging the heavy, dusty mailsacks was exhausting and monotonous. With the cancelling machines chattering away, the mailing section was a constant din of noise, deafening and enervating. Learning to toss mail into the cases without really looking demanded automatic precision. As Halper remembered, standing for eight hours in one place made the "eyes become slack," the face turn "dead." [24] Only hands and eyes remained alive. "I became a machine myself," he wrote, "tossing countless letters into square openings hour after hour." [25] Working seven nights a week, he went home at three in the morning, dead tired.

Although a civil service job offered almost certain security, sorting mail was deadening and dehumanizing, the kind of work that reminded Halper of life on Chicago's West Side. The job, he said later, was "almost intellectual suicide." He felt sorry for himself, but he also felt sorry for others. As he got acquainted with them, he listened to their stories, began to understand their moods and feelings. An interest in them helped him, in turn, to understand himself. After a while, he was transferred to the cashier's office, where he sold postage stamps under the big rotunda. His new assignment was a change of pace, but the monotony of the routine remained. He saw that a "year in the postal services in Chicago is worth a million dollars to the right person," but he also saw that the job was not for him. He had other plans.[26]

In the autumn of 1928, Marianne Moore, the editor of *Dial* magazine in New York, accepted one of his sketches and a short story. He was elated. On the very day that he was to have been promoted from substitute clerk to a regular clerkship with increased pay and permanent position, he resigned his job with the post office and never went back. There had been few gains: he had saved a little money; he had made a few acquaintances and listened to a few stories. But he no longer wanted to spend his life at the post office or in the kinds of jobs that had been his for the last seven or eight years. As he said later, "I always wanted to become a writer, but I could never work myself out of the rut of the dull, monotonous West Side streets and my dreary bread-and-butter labor." The acceptance of his story gave him the confidence he needed.[27]

In her letter Marianne Moore had written: "We like your story about the post office . . . and we're printing it. . . ."[28] He had, he felt, found his vocation at last. Members of his family did not agree; they tried their best to persuade him otherwise. His father, having given up his grocery store after the death of his wife, was lonely now and a little bewildered by his son's plans. His oldest brother urged him to try advertising; another brother in clothing urged him to join his company and become a correspondent, writing letters to the customers. He could not, he knew, reconsider a decision that had been in the making for such a long time. "I . . . left town the next morning," he wrote, "to burn my bridges, to get away from the gray West Side and my family, and to try, once and for all, to become a writer."[29] He boarded a bus and headed straight for New York.

CHAPTER 2

Young Writer in New York

WHEN Halper arrived in New York for the first time in the autumn of 1928, Coolidge-Hoover prosperity had already shown signs of weakening. An enormous confidence in government and business had carried prices of common stocks to unprecedented heights. Speculation had increased; business was faltering. Unemployment was a more serious problem with the recession of 1927 than at any other time since immediately after World War I. The summer of 1928, fast becoming a time of economic "hesitation" and financial uncertainty, found the stock market wavering and losing ground. Most Americans were busy with political conventions, with the upcoming election, with all the excitement over Al Jolson's new talking picture, *The Jazz Singer*.

In New York Halper's meager savings lasted only a few months. Of necessity, he returned to Chicago, where he found a job in a law office, researching deeds and mortages. During the spring and summer he saved nearly three hundred dollars, and in September, 1929, he headed back to New York. A month later the Wall Street crash plunged the country into its worst economic depression. Although signs for the future were hardly encouraging, he stayed East this time for good and set about becoming a published writer. He had just turned twenty-five.

Settling into a routine, he found the business of writing as demanding, difficult, and lonely as the life of a worker. But it was also different. In Chicago he had never been part of the sophisticated and intellectual life of the city, had never known those writers and artists who had drifted to New York and Paris and had become members of the lost generation. Experience had been a personal matter. He had learned about art and music and literature on his own; his chief concern had been with earning a living, mostly by manual labor. When he went to New York to make his way as a writer, his lonely and dreary life on Chicago's West Side had partly immunized him against the adversities that writers, especially in the beginning, sometimes encounter.

Liabilities of his West Side experience became assets. He had been schooled in the values and work habits of his lower middle-class Jewish family background; he had inherited a firm and unyielding belief in the individual and in man's capacities for hope and endurance. When he left Chicago, he not only realized his dream of leaving the West Side, but he also took his memories of the streets and factories and little shops on which he could now look with some affection, even love. With the stock market crash and the government's growing concern for labor problems and the welfare of workers, what Halper had always known as "life" had, ironically enough, become the growing concern both of history and literature.

But he had come to New York, not to follow some new trend or to espouse a cause, not even finally to escape a way of life; he had come to seek a new one, to pursue a hope and a dream. He wanted to write stories, to describe what he knew of life, not reform the world according to some new pattern. Malcolm Cowley's invitation to exiled artists to return and assist in the class struggle, a historical process, Cowley said, that was "vastly bigger than the individual," in no way applied to Halper. He had never been and never wanted to be a member of the lost generation. He had little interest in joining any organization that sought to further political and social causes. His interest lay in the individual's relationship to the changing business and industrial world that he had known in Chicago, and the individuals he meant were those "little" people who, like himself, had come from the shabby, poverty-stricken areas of the city and who were constantly confronting new ideas and changing patterns of life that the "historical process" generated. As he said later,

We writers of America live in a capitalistic society; some of us describe the hopes, faiths, and despairs of people who earn their daily bread in factories, stores, and offices; others of us describe the hopes and despairs of the middle class; still others of us describe the mores and the decay of the upper classes, and their hopes for the continuance of the *status quo*. Why not do away with labels and merely call ourselves commentators, or historians, of present-day society as we see it? That is less pretentious, it seems to me, and more truthful. [1]

In coming to New York, he set out to be both historian and artist; he wanted to set down what he knew of his own experience as truthfully and as effectively as possible.

I *Starting Out in New York*

Once in New York, Halper began the long and toilsome business of establishing himself as a writer. Friends helped him. He looked up a former co-worker from the post-office days in Chicago who now lived in Brooklyn and stayed for a while with him and his family. The family liked Halper, accepted his desire to write, urged him to go to left-wing meetings at Communist headquarters near Union Square, even tried to inveigle him into writing propaganda skits for the cause. He refused. Instead, he set about working in his own way, which meant working alone and working long hours. He began sending his stories to literary agents, who mostly returned them, and to the little magazines, which sometimes published them.

Contacts with magazines brought further leads. Meeting Elliot E. Cohen, editor of *The Menorah Journal*, which H. L. Mencken called the best-edited magazine in the country, proved fruitful and important. Cohen, a warm and talented graduate of Yale, devoted to Jewish interests, leaned to the left in his political thinking. As editor of *Menorah* and later of *Commentary* until his death in 1958, he was patron, mentor, and friend to Halper and to many struggling young writers. Accepting "Brothers Over a Grave" for publication, he invited Halper to his office, where they talked of writers and of writing. Of the eight stories that Halper published in 1929, Cohen printed three. His encouragement and acceptance of Halper's work was the kind of support a young writer needed. He did more. He introduced Halper to other writers, to Kenneth Fearing and Charles Reznikoff, to Clifton Fadiman, Louis Berg, and others, including a friend (Halper uses a fictitious name in identifying him) who in turn introduced him to Max Lieber, a new literary agent. His meeting with Lieber was a significant and fateful event that was to influence Halper's life for the next twenty years.[2]

An editor in Brentano's publishing house before it had been eliminated by worsening economic conditions, Lieber had taken book columnist Harry Hansen's advice and opened an author's agency. Lieber believed that "times were changing" and that the depression was "already producing a new type of writing, a different kind of author";[3] he accepted Halper as a promising client. Halper, less than enthusiastic, had hoped to be allied with an established agency, but all of them had turned him down. He needed an agent; he needed the advice, the assistance, and encouragement that an agent could give. He shared Lieber's admiration for Russian writers and listened to his

new agent's outspoken contempt for the blindness of the big magazines and publishers to "America's true economic and social condition." "Your time is coming," he told Halper.[4]

Trying to work in a cold room for long periods of time made
concentration difficult. Often Halper spent the day at the Public
Library, reading and thinking and making notes, not returning until
late in the evening to his room, where he sometimes continued
reading, still wearing his overcoat. He read steadily. He discovered
new Russian and continental writers. He read Fyodor Sologub,
Alexey Remizov, Ivan Turgenev, Pio Baroja, Thomas Mann, Mikhail
Lermontov.[5] He reread Nikolai Gogol's "Old World Landowners"
five times, "trying to discover the seed of his warmth, the secrets of
his superb technique at portraiture as he used seemingly innocuous
snippets of detail to limn the old couple in that tale."[6] He studied
Chekhov's "The Lady with the Dog" and Gogol's "The Overcoat"; he
discovered Henrik Ibsen and Gustave Flaubert, Ivan Alexeyevich
Bunin and Emile Zola. In pursuing his own "apprenticeship," he
studied the style and technique of the masters of their craft. Style
became a major concern.

Already he had begun to sort out and evaluate the usefulness of his
readings. The "one living writer" whom he greatly admired was
James Joyce, "a purist who writes classic English."[7] He liked Joyce's
early work best—*Dubliners* and *A Portrait of the Artist as a Young
Man*—and the early Hemingway. As he said later, "I still regarded *In
Our Time* the prime collection of American short stories
and *The Sun Also Rises* a masterpiece along with *The Great
Gatsby.* . . ."[8] He praised Sherwood Anderson: "he meant so much
to young writers, especially Chicago writers," for he showed all of
those who were tired of "machine-made literature" how to find the
knob in "the half light," how to open "the door a crack." He thought
Winesburg, Ohio and eight or ten "really great, great short stories"
gave Anderson a permanent niche in the literary hall of fame. "We all
learned from him, and we owe him an immense debt."[9] He liked
Ring Lardner's "wonderful slang," the deceptively simple design and
writing of his stories, which often disclosed "cracks in American life
over which the population keeps wheeling merrily along."[10] He
thought that Edna Ferber's "early short stories, which are really
entire novels crammed into five thousand words, comprise her best
work"; [11] that, although O. Henry wrote a few superb tales, most of
them are "tricky and mediocre." He listed Stephen Crane, the early
Erskine Caldwell, Katherine Anne Porter, William March, John

O'Hara, William Saroyan as having a "far better record." George Milburn's *No More Trumpets*, he thought, "is . . . one of the best volumes of short stories published in America." [12]

Sometimes he interrupted his working schedule. Since he could buy theatre and movie tickets at "ridiculously low prices" at Gray's Drug Store at 43rd Street and Broadway, he continued a pattern of life that had developed in Chicago. Among many others, he especially remembers Lee Tracy in *The Front Page* and the Marx brothers in *Animal Crackers*; some marvelous theatre with Lowell Sherman, Osgood Perkins, Alice Brady. He had made friends with artists, even painted a little himself; there were hours of talk about Van Gogh and Picasso, about Breughel and Bosch. He met young women, who sometimes stayed with him. He went to lectures and parties and walked the streets of New York and watched the crowds around Union Square. For the young writer finding his way, living in New York was a "wonderful, solitary life, and inexpensive. . . ." [13]

II *Young Writer at Work*

Halper's first few publications establish both the direction of his writing and his style. "Whites Writing up the Blacks," his first published sketch, is part factual observation, part interpretation; his ideas are both social criticism and good sense. In the one and one-half page statement, he makes his point about blacks that still rings true: he objects to those white writers who go South and gather or concoct "old faithful Joe" yarns and then publish them as authentic statements about Negroes. This country, he wrote in 1929, "has not produced one Negro capable of presenting a sincere picture of himself or his people." [14] He thought that as with any ethnic group, the white writer is still the spectator who "catches the rhythm, but cannot set the song down. . . ." [15] His observation defines his own program, for he himself had set out to catch the rhythm and song of people and places, to portray the inner life and thoughts of those individuals within the fairly narrow but typical experience that had been his own.

"Chicago Mail Clerks," his second published article, was the first of six essays and stories that he wrote in the next several years about his experience in the post-office. With the actual events still fresh in his memory, he traced the steps that led to getting his job as substitute mail-sorter on the night shift, the rules under which the workers functioned, and the effect on the individual as he mechanically sorted mail day after day. His language was informative and simple; his point of view, personal and realistic. Recognizing the agonized relation of man and machine, he noted the conditions of labor, the dusty air that all must breathe; the open lavatories and toilets, where privacy is never possible; the tyranny of a system that is faithfully and thoughtlessly carried out by well-meaning supervisors who are in turn supervised, each one trying to hang onto his job. He described man's battle with the machine in vivid terms that show how demeaning and forbidding the whole system had become and what debilitating effects it had on the workers. He does not, however, offer a plan of reform; his aim was other. Rather he exalted the "clerks," not as "proletarian" propaganda, but as individuals of dignity and worth who have tried to cope with the agony and pain of a monotonous job, have tried to keep their inner lives, their hopes and dreams intact.

To know the workers as individuals or in small groups where common interests made for candid talk and even friendship was to catch both their qualities and their weaknesses. Sometimes the job had become so competitive that they could not stand the strain. Sometimes blacks and whites, working so close together that physical contact was unavoidable, must become tolerant of each other or lose their jobs. A student in music found that his sense of harmony was literally being destroyed; he decided to leave. For some the place served as a retreat; a middle-aged man, once a proprietor of an ice-cream parlor, found that his wife was paying too much attention to the soda jerk. He got rid of the ice-cream parlor; when he could find no other work, he entered the postal service. Everyone had his own story and his own problems—the hoboes, the tramp printers, the sailors who had seen everything and done everything, yet still envied the "people in Fords and Packards."

In describing his experience at the post-office, Halper deals essentially with his own story, with highly personal material, not as social reformer or political activist, but as social commentator and as artist. His observations begin with objective description, deepen into the subjective life of the writer, broaden to include the personalities and private lives of his fellow workers. In catching the rhythm and song of men doing their jobs, the motion and meaning of man's relation to the machine, he uses a simple and familiar style that enables him to shape and heighten his material into an artistic representation of the remembered actuality. The vividness of his description permits the reader to see and hear the experience, to catch the rhythm and movement of the scene, to apprehend knowledge through feeling and sound and motion.

This relation between thought and rhythm and motion becomes a significant part of Halper's interest in art. In "White Laughter" (1931), a complex story that mingles memory of his post-office friends with his artist friends in New York and a feeling of transcendence that impels the spirit of laughter, he shows how controlled movement and rhythm lead to creative insight. Before talking about his artist friends, he remembers two workers from the post-office, Bart, a young Negro from Pontiac, Michigan, and his Indian friend John from South Dakota. The narrator-writer has learned something about his craft from both of them. From John he has learned about many gods; he has seen what it is to talk straight, stand strong, to see directly and think clearly.

From Bart he has learned that "tossing mail is a great art," and in describing the young Negro's ability, the narrator describes the artist's method in creating and shaping experience. As Halper says, recalling his own experience:

You stand in front of a case for eight hours and slowly your body dies until only your hands are alive. Your hands and your eyes. After the first half-hour you work up a sort of rhythm, your body sways a little, and you do not hear the hard chatter of more than a hundred canceling machines. You hear nothing. But you think a lot. Your thoughts are not important, everything seems slightly detached, and pretty soon, when your arms start throwing the mail very fast, one half of your brain falls asleep while the other half becomes so alive that nothing has to be explained to you.

As the young man hummed a tune, his body swaying in a rhythmical pattern, it "almost looked as if he was dancing." Fascinated, the narrator begins humming and swaying and asking, "How can a man dance standing still?" [16] The paradoxical question provides a descriptive key to Halper's own thinking: his awareness and sympathy for the ability of "little" people to catch the mystery and wonder in their job and in life around them.

"On the Shore," his first published short story, had used the same post-office material, even some of the same phrasing of "Chicago Mail Clerks," but he had charged the writing with an intensity of feeling and emotion. The story, told by a narrator, is about Halper's young Negro friend, Bart. They have been sorting mail on the same shift and have struck up a friendship. As work slackens, they go for walks together, heading off toward Michigan Avenue and the lake shore. Partly through talk and partly through silence in the gathering darkness, they come to a deeper understanding. "I cannot remember the words," the narrator writes, "but what he said went deep into me, as something warm and genuine." [17] Next day on the job they do not feel at ease with each other, and as the days pass, the tension between them lessens. In summer the narrator takes a leave of absence. When they say goodbye, "loneliness enveloped us, each separately. I caught it in his eye and knew that he saw it in mine." Their mutual insight into each other's inner thoughts, which had begun as a feeling of warmth and a sense "of space and water," has become conscious awareness of man's similarities. In a moment of mutual trust their hand shake affirms their earned knowledge "of the word brotherhood." [18]

"Chicago Mail Clerks" showed man's search for a place in a lonely, changing mechanical world; "White Laughter" shows his ingenuity at coping with that world through art and motion. "On the Shore" introduces another important theme that functions as a counter force to the mechanized world of urban life: the impelling and pervasive force of the natural world—the lake and wind, the sun and seasonal change—on man's life, a deep and abiding force that the artist Joan Miró recognizes as the "call of the earth." As the title of the story indicates, the narrator's response to human companionship takes place on shore in late spring and early summer, and this awareness of the natural world, of seasonal change, of earth's mysteries, and of man's need for reaching out in the world of wonder that lies about him reenforces the wisdom of compassion and sympathy and mutual love between man and his fellow creatures. The experience amounts to vision. The narrator walks along Jackson Boulevard: "Men, women, young girls in a hurry; the late sun covering sides of buildings, street cars going carefully, impatiently; the warm wind. Slowly I began to think of other things." [19] More than sentimental attachment to scenery and the calendar, Halper's response to the natural world is deep-seated and integral to his thinking, to the structure of his stories and novels, and to the motivation of his characters.

Inevitably he discovered new subject material. Perhaps his loneliness and his very real affection for his family were factors that turned his thinking to memories of his own past—as he says, "I suddenly became obsessed with my own family and background." [20] He began to reminisce, to think of stories and events. He recalled family differences, the idiosyncracies of individuals, family feuds and conflicts; he thought of relatives who came to visit and sometimes stayed; of "brothers who left home to live in a hotel." He thought of his father and mother, of their struggle with poverty and high ideals; of his mother's painful illness and death; of his father's grocery business and its steady decline; of his own youth on the cold gray West Side of a hustling city that exacted long hours of toil and steady endurance. But he also remembered his affection for his family, for people, for the city; for the long nights, the changing seasons, the noise and sound of the city that sometimes seemed like song; for all the experiences with family and jobs and a growing knowledge and awareness of people and places. This obsession with family and background and work experiences furnishes the material for most of his major work.

As he began to think about his past, patterns and scenes and personalities began taking shape in his imagination. "Brothers Over a Grave," which Elliot Cohen published under the heading "Commentaries" along with a piece by Tupper Greenwald, is typical of his direction. Clearly autobiographical and told by a narrator in the first person, the story recounts the visit of his several brothers to their mother's grave. As they stand in the cemetery with honest and sincere feelings to be expressed, they are confronted by a professional mourner who offers to "pray" for them because "my hand is paralyzed" and "I am an old poor man." The man actually begins to weep, but they do not engage him. When the brothers leave, they see the man again, this time slapping his arms, his "right arm . . . as active as his left." They drive away in silence to the "vacant, impersonal stare" of the professional mourner. For a while they "forgot they were salesmen"; the narrator no longer is "a bitter-minded clerk who wanted to strike at the disorder of life." [21] As death has given them a common bond, so the mourner has given them a view of the falseness of all professionals, including themselves.

Having found his material, Halper became preoccupied with his past, with Chicago, with setting down a number of stories about his family and growing up on the West Side. Some of these, like "Relatives," "The Goose Dinner," and "Hot Night on the West Side," were accepted by little magazines, but during 1929 he had published only eight essays and stories; in 1930, only six. At the same time, he had been at work on a novel about Chicago, which he called *Good-bye, Again*. Although publishers looked at it and some were even interested in it, his agent could not persuade anyone to publish it; the depression had made them cautious. Only part of *Good-bye, Again* has ever seen publication. Elliot Cohen liked the style and subject matter; he agreed to extract two sections from it and print them as short stories in *The Menorah Journal*. "Memorial" and "Young Writer, Remembering Chicago" show a growing control of subject material and a mastery of technique.

"Memorial" is the story of five sons and their father, who go to the synagogue to listen to the Kaddish prayer for the dead intoned for their mother. As the five sons sit together, "looking solemn, two married, three single, all Americans, all anxious to get ahead, one a little cracked, the one who wrote stories," it is clear that they are hardly listening to the service. Even Dave, the narrator, watches his father's face as it grows "kind and lonely looking," and finds himself praying for "his mother and for himself, for all the stories he had tried to write, for wasted days and for all the nights he had lain awake in his New York room, for those moments when everything in life seemed sad and beautiful." As his thoughts wander more to himself than to his mother and the prayer ends, he sees his father go to the rabbi and offer money, but the rabbi refuses. "He said two dollars was a joke." [22] One of the older brothers understands and gives him five. Back home listening to the rain and in quite different circumstances, Dave truly realizes that the loss of his mother is the lonely shape that haunts his mind. Highly autobiographical and vividly real, "Memorial" demonstrates Halper's ability to give such ordinary events an intensity of feeling and meaning. In the stories about his family that follow, he is mostly consistent in making Dave the narrator and calling his older brothers Ben and Milt.

"Young Writer, Remembering Chicago" breaks new ground. Since its publication, it has become his best known and most respected story. Written in language that is lyrical and poetical, a style that is part stream-of-consciousness and part sensitive reporting, it is a very personal account of his thoughts and feelings and appreciation of his city. Using short, sometimes fragmentary sentences, he probes into his feelings of fear and terror, of pain and suffering, of loneliness and dreamy longing. His reactions and thoughts are organized according to the seasons of the year. The story begins with the fall, which may be the real beginning of life in the city, extends through winter and spring, and ends in summer. In remembering these early years on Chicago's West Side, he relates his own growing up to the seasons, to the rhythms and songs of the wind that howls and blasts in the fall and winter and brings the moist damp air of spring, the glaring heat of summer. Blowing and blowing, it seems to shape the life of the city.

To remember Chicago was to remember his own life. His memories of "Fall" were the memories of beginnings, his youth, the poverty and places, the dreams and stories of childhood. "Winter" brought memories of work at the foundry, of seeing a black man shot to death. "Spring" erupted with primitive force, sending him into the streets, into the warm winds caressing inner desires. In "Summer" he walked the streets and parks, working at his night job in the post office, remembering people and the many jobs he could not forget. "I am sorry in the summer," he writes, "for many things, for those hot nights of open air dancing that had to fade, for the fall that is coming. And for all the gray dead things in life, the things that drag themselves slowly along, I am sorry." [23]

With its slangy rhythms and poetical phrasing, "Young Writer, Remembering Chicago" expresses the private thoughts of an individual, but in its careful observation and sensitive understanding of people and places, their joys and losses, it captures at the same time the inner thoughts and feelings of the city. Well received by critics and anthologized by editors, the story was selected by Kathleen Tankersley Young for inclusion in the pamphlet series that she brought out for Modern Editions Press in 1932. Halper revised it and reentitled it "Chicago Side-Show," and Louis Lozowick's illustration of a cityscape called "Avenue" served as frontispiece. Later, after further revisions, the story became a major part of *On the Shore*.

III *Marking Time*

As the economic depression deepened, Halper continued to write, living with friends in the Bronx now and maintaining himself on a minimum budget. Despite the failure of his first novel, his agent had advised him to try writing a second one. Elliot Cohen, just as encouraging, offered help of a different kind. Cohen persuaded Clifton Fadiman, an editor at Simon & Schuster, to recommend Halper for a residency at Yaddo, the rent-free artist's colony at Saratoga Springs, New York, where he spent the summer of 1930.

Yaddo, a haven for artists of all kinds, enabled a person to work at ease and live in splendor on the large estate. Meals were elegantly served, with tea every afternoon at four. Halper found the place delightful, with the great pine trees and sloping lawns, and in this atmosphere of leisure and freedom, he worked well, making progress on his second novel and enjoying conversations with such fellow artists as Winthrop Sargeant, Aaron Copland, Leonard Ehrlich, Paul Bowles. As he listened to their arguments over established writers and artists, he felt that he had "acquired a small foothold in the world of letters." But he also discovered that writers and musicians and sculptors differed little from foundry workers or young punks in a mail-order house in their comments and criticisms about each other. At Yaddo, he said, "I gradually felt the rough edges of my Chicago background being sanded away." [24]

Even though he finished his novel and was hopeful, his return to New York in September, 1930, seemed a dreary business. Max Lieber, enthusiastic about the novel, was unable to do more than get the publishers to read it. They would not buy. There were other problems; as the autumn dragged on, writing became more and more difficult. The arrangement for living with his two artist friends in the Bronx was no longer tenable. Striking out on his own, he rented a three-room unheated tenement flat on East 11th Street, not far from Union Square. The new environment gave new perspectives, and with the change came a renewed vitality that did not last.

Although he had worked constantly for two years, he had published only a handful of stories in little magazines. The winter of 1930–31, he recalls, seemed endless. Partly out of curiosity, he occasionally went to a left-wing political rally or watched the action in Union Square. Once, he remembers, he and Kenneth Fearing went to the *New Masses* annual ball at Webster Hall, across the Street from his flat. He heard Diego Rivera speak at a meeting of the John Reed Club. As the depression continued and interest in social reform grew, Max Lieber, Elliot Cohen and others tried to interest him in the Communist Party and political propaganda. Although he had read and studied Karl Marx and other Communist writers and even thought that the Communist Party was "the prime potent voice raised during the thirties," he was more irritated than impressed with "their repeated shouts and emotional appeals for change. . . ." [25] He had come to New York to write, and while he had little money and the economic situation worsened, he had no reason to change his direction. "Never having known affluence in the good times of the past," he was not unprepared to cope with poverty and economic insecurity. Nor was he indifferent to the worst depression that he or most people had ever known, but he was determined to stick to his independent ways and to his dream of writing.

Still depressed over the novels he had written that did not sell and over the stories he wanted to write and could not, he began typing out a long satire—around thirty thousand words—of Ernest Hemingway, a parody in part of *A Farewell to Arms*, which he had admired when it came out but no longer liked. "A Farewell to the Rising Son," with its long subtitle "A Novel of Love and Sacrifice along the Heroic Polish Frontier," is like no other story that Halper was to publish. Farcical and funny, but neither vicious nor malign, the story is closer to raillery and banter than slander and calumny. Much of the fun lies in the exaggeration of phrasing that imitates Hemingway's style and in the absurd action and talk of the characters. The writing is never brilliant; it is sometimes clever. In a note from "THE AUTHOR," Halper advises that "None of the characters of this book are alive. Most of them are dead but don't know it." [26]

"A Farewell to the Rising Son" is narrated by Lieutenant John Thomas, an American serving with the Polish forces in Poland. The fighting has stalled; the men are waiting around. "That spring" Thomas and Captain Pikowski, a tall good-looking fellow who comes from a fine old Polish family, "lived in a small town near a long narrow lake, and the mountains, blue and cold, lay behind us." They walk and talk quite a lot, skip rocks, and chase crows. Lt. Thomas tightens his belt a great deal, blames the war in a vague sort of way for his situation, and often lapses into periods of silence. They are easily entertained; the General's parrot, who curses them in Polish, furnishes endless amusement. The episode fairly typifies the writing:

Pilowski laughed. I laughed. Both of us laughed. We felt better. Then we thought of the war. We stopped laughing. We walked along, the moonlight shining on our snug fitting Polish uniforms and I wondered if I belonged to a lost generation. When we reached the shore of the lake we stopped to look at the dark heaving water. Pikowski stared into the darkness for a long time. I placed my hand on his shoulder. It was the war again. I did not say anything. [27]

The affair with the General's niece, Sakarine Kowalka, is sheer buffoonery. Sakarine and Lt. Thomas meet at a window, and she asks him to come inside. Halper writes:

The war was here, but I went inside. It didn't matter. Nothing mattered. The front was a long ways off. Maybe I would get killed. Miss Kowalka reached down, gripped my hand firmly and I swung my body through the open window. It was better that way. I did not have to go through the door in the conventional manner. I was not much for conventions anyway. [28]

In a few days, Thomas is ordered to the front, and as he gets off his horse to tighten the saddle strap, Sakarine appears for a scene of farewell.

At first the war goes well. They win a victory, go to Spain for a short vacation, return to Poland to fight another battle; they win another victory and go on another vacation, this time to Paris. Here Lt. Thomas meets a Lady Cynthia, who falls in love with him but realizes that it is no good. "It is the war," Lt. Thomas tells her, as he buckles his belt a little tighter. When he returns to Poland, Sakarine Kowalka is still waiting. Before he goes to the front, they have an affair.

In three months the stage is set for a big advance, but the war goes badly. The Germans break through, Thomas is hit in the arm, the snow begins to fall, and the big retreat is on. As the retreat turns into a rout, Pilowski is killed, and Lt. Thomas escapes over the bridge, just before it is blown up. When he awakens, he is in the hospital.

As luck will have it, Sakarine works in the hospital as a kind of helper. The surgeon repairs his arm; his recovery is nicely under way when Sakarine tells him that she is pregnant. Lt. Thomas buckles his belt, and the two of them escape from the hospital in a troika. They strike out for Finland, crossing the boundary into the city of Viborg on the eighth day. At the hospital the doctor tells him that Sakarine must have surgery. Lt. Thomas analyses their situation and declares that the trouble is they have "brought so much courage to this world." [29] Courage is exactly what they need, for instead of "winner take nothing," the winner learns that Sakarine is not only recovering nicely but that she has also given birth to twin boys. His reflection is an ironic non sequitur: "Outside the snow was falling quietly and I knew I belonged to a lost generation." [30] Having won so much, he surely does. The mean gray life of Chicago's West Side had never been this romantic.

Richard Johns, editor of *Pagany*, paid Halper $180 for the story. Since his living expenses came to around eight dollars a week, he could keep going on this for quite a while. By late spring, with his writing at a standstill and money running low, he had a bit of luck. He ran into a friend whom he had known at Yaddo and who was going to work at an adult summer camp, a fairly exclusive place in the Adirondacks at Warrensburg, New York. Halper liked the idea, sent in his application, and was taken on as a waiter and as a writer of skits. He returned to New York after the Labor Day week-end with enough money to last six months.

IV *On Writing*

"Writing," Halper said in 1944, "is a very, very personal business—I mean serious writing. It is like loving, or praying." [31] Being personal did not exclude the toilsome work of putting it all on paper; he outlined, rewrote, polished. What he means by personal emerges in that first published essay, "Whites Writing up the Blacks." His essential point is that any writer must know his material, must write only what he truly knows and feels. This insistence on honesty of thought and feeling guides and shapes his own work and serves as a yardstick for evaluating his fellow writers as he constantly read and studied.

Essentially a writer of the 1930's, he was admittedly influenced by the Depression, by the strikes and violence that characterized his world, by ideologies that dominated the thinking of the era, by his own experiences on Chicago's West Side. But he remained singularly free of ideological cant; he never joined the Communist party; he was not even a good fellow traveler. When he traveled, he traveled alone, following literary not political traditions and seeking a revolution of the human spirit more than a revolution of political and social power.

All artists, he believed, are influenced by the past, by the works especially of those whom the individual greatly admires. Original writers or artists or even cabinet makers, he thought, do not exist. Even Dostoevski was influenced by Gogol; the painter Breughel by his master Hieronymus Bosch.[32] "Great books," he wrote in 1932, "are novels of conflict, primarily, of friction between characters and ideas (Dostoevski); and where else in American life can be found such sharp contrasts as between European Jewish parents and their American-born children?" Family conflicts have already been written about, he said, "but always the friction has been portrayed by the writing of shallow bickerings, without a sense of warmth and understanding."[33] Some of the most sensitive and understanding novels had, he believed, come from Russian writers; he studied Gogol, Tolstoi, Turgenev. "The reading of a great novel makes you soar," he said. "It makes something inside of you sing."[34]

He admitted that his Jewish heritage was important; the Jewish writer is different, he thought, simply because he is Jewish. His own family life and his early training had been steeped in the traditional values and beliefs of his Jewish religious upbringing, in the awareness of being part of a minority group. During the years preceding World War II, such differences became strikingly apparent. As he said in 1944, "the betrayal of the Jews is part of the whole stinking hypocritical betrayal of the world."[35] The sensitivity of being a Jewish writer had, he thought, helped him—as it had any minority writer or person—to understand the "terrifying deadliness" of the "pogrom against human decency" that was taking place in America against

Jews and blacks and against poor people of any race or color or creed. Being Jewish helped one to "smell" out the contours of the present situation just as Kafka sensed "fascism" in Europe as far back as 1919.

In "Notes on Jewish-American Fiction," his single long piece of literary criticism, he assesses the Jewish-American literary situation in the early 1930's. It was, he thought, far from optimistic. The fault lay not so much with incompetence as with cowardice, and in his analysis he tells us something of his own thoughts about writing. "Small books which skim the surface of things," he said, are "safer, by far, to write" than the big book that "must be well planned and studied" and demands "all the labor, all the genuine feeling, every ounce of conscious literary strength and ability that the author posses-ses. . . ." [36] The novels of Jewish writers have become stereotyped and repetitive. Early writers established a pattern with the "immi-grant novels"—"young hopeful girls with shawls over their heads; eager, zealous men who stumbled off the ships expecting to find gold on the streets, then were led to the dark East Side tenements to suffer disillusion." Only Abraham Cahan's *The Rise of David Levinsky* (1917) towers above the many versions of the immigrant story. Cahan's novel "has undeniable power," he thought, "but insufficient force to transpose us back a few decades." [37] The ghetto tale quickly passed through the pioneer stage with a few authentic and forceful stories such as Fannie Hurst's *Humoresque* (1919) or Anzie Yezier-ska's *Hungry Hearts* (1920) and *Salome of the Tenements* (1922). Since "ghetto stories sold the fastest and took the high money," writers began turning them out. The East Side Tenements of New York—never some place in the South or West—invariably provided the setting. The story itself became stereotyped, "an overly colorful picture of bearded men and mothers, of sacrifice so that little Hyman could continue with his violin lessons, or Deborah with her writing; at other times the rise of a line of merchants." [38]

The initial stories of Hurst and Yezierska were excellent; when they switched to other themes, they failed to live up to their early promise. The peddler novels of Elias Tobenkin presented America as a land of golden opportunities, but imitators turned the idea into the "search-relentless theme," and Ludwig Lewisohn, certainly an "above the average Jewish-American writer," used it to advantage in *The Island Within* (1928), then repeated it with variations in subse-quent novels.

A group of new writers, Halper believed, were using a new approach: they were not trying "to glorify the American Jew, or tear him down." Seeking new materials and writing with honesty and sincerity, they were trying to "put down, understandingly, only what they see and really feel." They avoided sentimentality and the old "search-relentless" and ghetto themes. Myron Brinig in *Singermann* (1929) described a Jewish family in a Northwestern mining town; Charles Reznikoff in *By the Waters of Manhattan* (1930) described immigrants in New York who do not succeed; Lawrence Drake in *Don't Call Me Clever* (1929) told a story of brothers and a shady deal; only Michael Gold in *Jews Without Money* (1930), often maudlin and sentimental, revived the "old faithful-son-and-mother situations." Having "thrown overboard" the "old hooey and melodrama," these new writers have written about "real people, real characters, folks who do not weep or laugh at the pressure of buttons employed by the older authors." [39]

The wider Jewish-American scene, Halper thought, had hardly been touched. "In almost every family when the parents are foreign-born," he thought, "there is material for a meaty novel." [40] Many themes had been neglected: the isolation of the Jew in the small town; the relation of Southern blacks and poor whites to the Jews; the plight of the Jewish traveling man; or the problem of the young Jewish man who has become lost in the city trying to make good. But exploring the problems of the Jewish minority, he said later, was less important than dealing "honestly with the time in which we are living . . ."; in the final analysis, "a writing man is a man first or he isn't one." [41]

From his own writing, Halper had learned that the formula for good writing did not exist. The best stories, he believed, were those written about "real" people, and although every writer must make his own discoveries, he found that the best "characters" were those who meant something to him. *"I write about people who have been eating me for years.* These people may be friends, relatives, enemies, or people I used to work with a long time ago." In offering specific examples, he comes close to the theory of Henry James in "The Art of Fiction."

They may be persons I saw only for a second while traveling in a bus, while descending into the subway, or while eating in a cafeteria. They may be my brothers, my sister. All right. Something they did, or said, some way they looked, smiled, sobbed or grunted, some gesture they made, some act of selfishness or generosity, made their character, or characteristics, stick in my mind, the *clicking, writer's part of my mind,*

the part he calls the "deep honesty of self." [42]

Then begins the lonely process of writing, of shaping the material with honest intention. As the original prototypes are "fictionalized" into characters, they may be enlarged or foreshortened, heightened or intensified until they become "more real than they were in actual life." [43] In writing about real people, a writer may, of course, run into objections; the prototype may still be recognizable. Halper's family were, and they voiced complaints. Why "do you always write about us?" What could he say? They were his background, his point of view; in writing about his own experience, in collecting and shaping the only materials that he had known, his choices were limited and inevitable.

He did not write about the struggling masses because he did not know them. He did not write about the proletariat because he did not know what the word really meant. Rather, he set out to impose his will on his own past, to write about his family, about people he had known in factories and shops, not as historical process or labor propaganda, not even as ethnic groups or political bias, but as human beings with human needs and problems and desires. Although he believed in social reform, as a writer his aim was other. In striking at the disorder of life, he wanted to catch the song and rhythm, the inner life of the people and city that he knew and loved. As he says of his friend in the Post Office, he wanted to catch the dance of man standing still.

CHAPTER 3

Striking at Disorder: Union Square

UNION SQUARE was not the first novel Halper had written, but
the fourth. His first novel, *Good-bye, Again*, from which Elliot
Cohen had extracted the two stories already discussed in Chapter 2,
had been praised but rejected by the editors at The Viking Press. His
second novel, *Windy City Blues*, had caused more stir, and he recalls
that several publishers all but accepted it before the editors at Viking,
his last hope, decided against it. With the book market depressed, no
publisher wanted to take a chance with material that was, as his agent
told him, too experimental. Writing to Marshall Best, editor at
Viking, Halper admitted that, although he still believed in the novel,
it had become a "white elephant." He now thought that if he had
written it in straight prose, the "book would have been accepted long
ago." Later he tried several times to revise it, but never successfully.
Before he shelved it, twenty-two publishers had rejected it.[1]

The editors at Viking, still interested in his work, had already
encouraged him by asking that he try a third novel, which they also
rejected. But when Marshall Best saw the plan for *Union Square*, he
felt certain that it had all the earmarks of a winner. The long apprenticeship for that "young fellow who's always typing hard at something
or other," had ended.[2] His persistence and patience attest a confidence in self that reflects the values and belief that give enduring
strength to his writing.

I *Writing* Union Square

Ironically, Halper's first published novel was not about Chicago,
but New York. Yet in writing about the "sights, people and events
that he was seeing daily" in his own neighborhood—11th to 14th
Streets, including Union Square—he had changed neither his style
nor his attitudes. What he says about his method is applicable to most
of his work:

Against this strident, viciously competitive background, I have thrown the figures of my novel. Most of the main characters are drawn from life. The book was written, to state the matter baldly, in privation, loneliness and desperation, and was generated by a certain grimly humorous mood which I suppose was more or less of a reflex action from my surroundings.[3]

Those surroundings provide both a geographical setting and a historical framework for the novel.

Union Square, as Leonard Q. Ross remembered it in 1939, was a mixture of shapes. "The park itself, an oval set within the square," he writes, "is like an elongated wheel with six spokes. The spokes are wide walks, each leading to the tall flagpole in the center, which was put up in 1926 by the Tammany Society in honor of that celebrated statesman, Boss Murphy." [4] The inscription in capital letters around the base of the pole is from Thomas Jefferson: "How little do my countrymen know what precious blessings they are in possession of and which no other people on earth enjoy." Trees bordered the walk; an iron rail fence tried to preserve the grass. In 1939 men loafed and read and slept on the wooden benches that lined the walks. At the South end of the Square stood the statue of George Washington seated on a huge bronze horse.

By the 1930's the Square had already become a synonym for the down and out, for riots and social activists, for wild-eyed social ideas and economic upheaval. The place was a polyglot of nationalities, a clash of ideologies, a roar of violent and chaotic action; in its honest and genuine concern for betterment, it had always been American to the core. Later, Halper wondered why no one had ever written about it, for he saw that it was a vague and shadowy barometer of coming events which were to alter the direction of social and political and economic thought during the 1930's. The Square contained, he thought, the shape of history passing as revue.

Much of history during the 1930's recorded the loneliness and despair of the people. Edmund Wilson, writing in 1931, defined man's condition in terms of losses:

What we have lost is, it may be, not merely our way in the economic labyrinth but our conviction of the value of what we were doing. Money-making and the kind of advantages which a money-making society provides for money to buy are not enough to satisfy humanity—neither is a system like ours in which everyone is out for himself and devil take the hindmost, with no common purpose and little common culture to give life stability and sense.[5]

The loneliness and desperation of the early 1930's, unlike that of the 1920's and the existential loneliness of the post World War II era, came from economic want as well as moral enervation.

The economic labyrinth was terrifying. In 1929 the annual average wage was less than $1500. By 1930 nearly six million people were unemployed. Although by 1932 the estimates ran from eight and a half to seventeen millions, the official figure was at a little more than twelve million or 24.9 percent of the labor force. No one was quite certain of the correct figure. Compared to their 1929 level, salaries in 1932 had dropped 40 percent; dividends, over 55 per cent; wages, 60 percent. Business losses ran from five to six billion dollars. Bread lines, Hoovervilles, homeless people sleeping in parks and going the rounds of restaurants, hitch-hiking on the highways, drifters of all ages and of both sexes, constituted "everyday" existence. In 1933 an estimated million transients were on the move. If Halper's mood were grimly humorous, the mood of history was likewise grim.

In the autumn of 1931, Rudy Vallee, appearing in George White's *Scandals*, sang to the audience that "life is just a bowl of cherries." Few people thought so. The bread lines were already lengthening. In the summer of 1932, army troops under the direction of Douglas MacArthur and Dwight D. Eisenhower, routed the bonus marchers in the nation's capital and frightened thoughtful citizens everywhere. Unemployment, business losses, poverty, and fear had begun to generate new social ideas, new economic demands, new political awarenesses. When England went off the gold standard, the shock weakened American banking and business. Many people believed that only the federal government was strong enough to promote the general welfare, even if federal intervention seemed foreign to the American way and signified a drift toward the welfare state.

On his return to New York from the summer camp in the Adirondacks in September, 1931, Halper grew more and more depressed by his situation. For a few days he worked with a director on a movie about Nazi Germany, but the project had to be abandoned when funds were not forthcoming. Living still in his tenement flat on East 11th Street, he felt little like working. Although some of his stories had been placed with H. L. Mencken, probably the best editor in America, the achievement was not enough. As an older writer at Yaddo had once told him, "there's nothing like a book to put you over." [6]

One day, shortly after his return, while walking along Fourteenth Street and listening to the "racket of Union Square," he "suddenly . . . saw a fellow walking backwards at a rapid and sure-footed pace." As he recalls, "the sight of The Man Who Walks Backwards, for some reason or other, galvanized me into action." Although he had walked the Square a thousand times, the scene had never before suggested itself "as material for a novel." [7]

As he headed back to his flat, he had come to a decision. Why not write about the place where he had been living and about the life of the Square? Almost at once the novel began taking shape; he wanted to "make the book lyrical, jazzy, almost like a revue—but with a cohesive, collective story line to cement the whole thing together." [8] He started taking notes and making outline after outline. As scenes and events began falling into place, he typed a résumé of the projected novel and sent it to Max Lieber. Within a week, after Lieber had forwarded it to Marshall Best, the editor at Viking, Best sent him a contract.

After three months of "fussing with outlines and notes" as he tried to figure out a way to "ensnare the complex swirl of sights, sounds and smells of Union Square," he finally started writing. [9] By May, 1932, part of a first draft was ready for the publishers, but he also saw that changes were needed, especially in the characters. He reconceived the artist Leon, changing him from a hunchback to a person shy and sensitive. He made the two Russians Vanya and Natasha less prominent, but did not associate them with either communistic causes or party politics. He added the barber, Mr. Franconi, giving him a significant and tragic role. As he neared the end of the novel, the fire scene became a problem. He did not want it to become "movie melodrama" or seem "untrue" as he sometimes felt it was. He even considered removing it altogether. Then, one evening as he was returning to his flat, he saw that the tenement building next to his own was on fire. With no intention of being heroic, he ducked into his own building, grabbed his manuscript and typewriter, and slipped out. His writing problem had been solved. In the final version the fire scene remains, the description of an actual event that he had experienced.

Halper completed *Union Square* by early summer of 1932 in time for fall publication, but good news necessitated a delay. Late in the summer, the Literary Guild chose the novel for its March selection, and in deference to the book club's decision, Viking delayed publication until early spring. When it finally appeared—officially on March

6, 1933—the timing could not have been worse. On Saturday, March 4, 1933, when Franklin Delano Roosevelt was sworn in as the thirty-second President of the United States, every bank in the country had closed its doors. People were near panic. Roosevelt assured a radio audience of millions of frightened listeners "that the only thing we have to fear is fear itself." But the fear and loneliness had already become part of the growing anxiety and frustration of an entire country groping for answers. Writing with the close observation that had characterized his shorter pieces, Halper portrayed that fear, that loneliness, that desperation in an assortment of individuals who lived near Union Square, and he described the Square and sometimes their lives with a lyrical sympathy and an ironic candor that also revealed the economic and moral losses that beset a generation. *Union Square* is the story of man's condition, dramatized as a jazzy, swift-moving revue.

II Union Square

Although *Union Square* tells the story of a number of individuals, no one person is truly its hero. Rather, the real hero may be the Square itself, the place as well as the people who tramp its streets, the collective relation of generic man to his surroundings. Like man, the Square has a double nature; for six days a week the periphery of the Square is a feud of nationalities, a tangle of lives, a storm of noise, a bedlam of business, a carnival of desperation. "But," as Halper writes,

within the square itself, it's quiet. A few bums and seedy unemployed sit huddled on the benches, staring at the cliffs of buildings, gazing at the sea of passing heads. From a cold, gray sky a wind comes sniffing at their bones. 4%, says the sign over the Amalgamated Bank. The flavor lasts.

And the flagpole, like a tremendous carpet tack, sticks its point into the windy sky.[10]

As the chaos of the outside suggests frantic desperation, so the inner square—the bums, the cold wind, the 4% interest rate—ironically suggests the lifeless, enervated inner being of man. As Edmund Wilson has said, life seemed without stability, without sense, without humanity; it had lost its common purpose.

The Square has further implications that are social and philosophic in meaning. James Nicholson, the demented printer, sees the place as a geographical center that is linked with the world beyond. "Union Square," Halper has him write,

is surrounded on all sides by mountains. To the north are the Alps, to the east the Caucasus, to the west lie the Urals, while southward stand the Ozarks, with the plains of Texas just beyond. And south, further still, lies the heavy sea, which heaves and rolls like oil. (3)

As philosopher-historian, Nicholson functions as a link with the past, a link that Halper sees as essential to understanding man's condition. Serving as a kind of Greek chorus throughout the novel, the old printer describes the Square in wasteland imagery that connects seasonal change with fate:

There are no trees, no beds of flowers. Seasons roll round like huge wagon wheels, each spoke a month, each revolution a year; the thick, fat hubs are as stolid as fate.
This is a land of waste and doom. The cold comes when the night falls and the wind rides on a storm. (5)

As the Square symbolizes man's superficial activities as well as his inner restiveness, so it stands as the collective statement of the social attitudes and spiritual values of an era.

Union Square is the pilgrimage of man through the early years of the Depression, the portrayal of the human comedy at a fixed place in a moment of crisis. Whatever abstract patterns the Square suggests, its essential vitality—or lack of it—derives from the people who inhabit it. The classifications are timeless: the parade of beggars, the legless, the blind, the ex-soldiers; the vendors, hawking their wares in traditional fashion; the places of entertainment—the movie, the burlesque, the taxi-dancing jazz bands; law and order in the person of Officer McGuffy; women gathering food and fuel in "ancient lots" or hanging up their washing; men listening to the radio voices of the "leaders of our country," who urge staunch and brave people to face "this severe and prolonged crisis" (107). Here the eternal prophet and orator addresses his fellow workers and comrades, haranguing them with a vision and an ideal of a newer and richer future. *Union Square* is the past forever being overthrown; the future forever being coaxed into existence. It is the vortex of change; it is America in transition.

Into the brick and mortar of city life, the natural world works its inexorable will, appearing as wind, sun, shadow, often as image or metaphor, assuming a role as city park or seaside, contributing to the organizational pattern of the novel as it had in some of the short stories. *Union Square* begins in autumn in part One, moves into early winter in parts Two and Three. In parts Four and Five, introducing a technique that he uses in later novels, he shows the reactions of individual characters to a single day, to Christmas and to the coming New Year. In part Six, still in winter, the big communist demonstration and a tenement fire sweep the characters along in events that are as impersonal and, like "fat hubs," as stolid as fate. The coming of the New Year has brought both success and defeat, both despair and hope. The "chill and bitter wind" that blows westward in the Square signifies a future of poverty as well as abundance, of endurance as well as hope. Man's only real assurance for the future lies in the inevitability of change, and here Halper means not only seasonal, but also social and economic, moral, and intellectual change.

Union Square begins and ends with a riot, but the novel is neither a revolutionary tract nor a sermon on economics. Just as the "wind rides on a storm," followed by a period of quiet in the natural world, so Union Square is "calm after the riot." Then the wind rises and shifts and bears down finally in an eruption of nervous frustration that leads to a clash of wills, the desperation of hopeful endurance. *Union Square* is filled with social protest, but the protest follows no prescribed theory or pattern of necessity. Rather, protest is made and implied through descriptive statements and satirical comment on events. In parts Two, Four, Five, and Six, the narrator describes a sale day in the Square, especially those in the New Year when business is booming; the contrasting quiet of Christmas morning; the change of weather from rain to snow after the big riot. In parts One and Two the manuscript of printer Nicholson voices the protest; in part Four, Officer McGuffy. Perhaps the bulk of the protest stems from the thought and feelings and actions of individuals, whose lives cross in sometimes purposeful, sometimes casual relationships, during that relatively calm period between two violent outbreaks. In portraying how each enacts his role of salesman or artist, of writer or freight handler, policeman or barber, bohemian, capitalist, communist, panhandler, Halper makes the decisions and feelings, the jealousies and betrayals of individuals serve as visible statement of the social, economic, the moral and intellectual life that makes up the web of history. Halper's characters play a double role that is both private and public, both personal and universal.

Although the Square serves a collective purpose, the novel focuses on the ten or twelve individuals who live in Twenty-Door City tenements and Glen Cove apartments. Their problems are more

personal than public—the amount of money a story brings, the
quantity of gin consumed, the acceptance of a painting, the mood of a
mistress. They are beset by fears, plagued by losses—the loss of
work, of wages, of a friend, of talent, of communication, of feeling,
of love, even of nerve. Indeed, life for most of the people is a matter of
losses, and while the losses are personal, they are also losses of an era.

For some, like Jason Wheeler, the losses are those of direction, of
confidence, of self-respect. Ex-poet and ex-communist, Wheeler is
still applauded for the poetry that he once wrote and for the promise
that he seems incapable of fulfilling. He has turned to drink and dope
and to writing pot boilers for cheap sex story magazines which pay
very little. A major character, if not a hero, he has remained in contact
with members of the party, but he has become disillusioned with
their aims and methods. Ill and depressed, he maintains an independent attitude and insists on an individual's honesty and sincerity.

Much of Halper's evaluation of the artist's relation to party politics
and activism is revealed through Wheeler's observations. The big
Party meeting at Webster Hall is dominated by speeches from young
intellectuals who follow the party line and harangue the listeners with
jargon and high-sounding slogans. Wheeler knows many of the speakers, knows something of their frustrations and failures. One, a young
writer from a well-to-do family, had returned from abroad to become
a comrade. "Years ago he had written modernistic verse, had lived in
Paris for a while, had learned to drink, to look bored, to feel himself as
belonging to the 'lost generation,' and had gone heavy for the Dada
acrobatics (274)." His language and his thinking are affected and false.
The most sensible speech comes from a young miner, who speaks
with "simple words" and smiles and gives honest evaluations. The
workers recognize the sincerity of the man. As speaker after speaker
mounts the platform, Jason wonders why "communists make their
meetings last so long . . ." (278).

The meeting at the Kremlin, the large tenement building that has
been remodeled into studios for young artists, is more bohemian than
political. Most of the people fancy themselves devoted to social
causes and political action; much of the poetry being read has a
"proletarian" slant. Nearly all have admired Jason Wheeler's satiric
attacks on the social system, but in asking for his criticism of their
poetry, they do not mean that he should attack them. Reflecting
Halper's own point of view, Wheeler accuses these would-be
proletarian writers of faddism. He tells them: "Fifteen or twenty

years ago you would, if you had been born earlier, been living in Greenwich Village, fighting for the 'new freedom,' free love, and all that sort of stuff "(287). Now the onetime "new" has become old hat. Every clerk believes in free love and in freedom. What the Revolution needs, he tells them in a long speech, is "militant workers, militant, intelligent workers." He reminds them that the young mine-worker was able to electrify the crowd because he "really feels what he's fighting for. He cares nothing about the latest ideology, nothing about Marxism, but he knows he's up against starvation and exploitation and eviction and he's putting up a battle" (287).

Jason castigates the young artists with ironic mockery. No artist, he tells them, becomes a proletarian poet just because he learns a few slogans and catch words like "*opportunism, capitalism, Leninism, the proletarian state, revolutionary, petty bourgeoisie . . .*" (286). Being radical isn't something new; the writer may not even find it useful. If a writer really wants to help the movement, Jason tells them, "you must first be capable in your craft (292)." Art that springs directly from a worker's life is one thing; "Manhattanized communism" is another. Jason—and Halper—readily accept the person with "real talent" who "knows what the struggle is all about and can translate it effectively through his medium." But as Jason says, "this country has produced no first-rate proletarian writers or artists, it has produced few enough second-raters" (293). Halper's emphasis on craftsmanship and his belief that good art is more useful than propaganda links him rather with the tradition of Mark Twain and Henry James and James Joyce than with that of Michael Gold and V. F. Calverton.

To most of the other characters, life becomes a matter of personal frustration, of moral and physical sickness. Wheeler's best friend, artist Leon Fisher, is less devoted to communist doctrine than to Comrade Helen, and Comrade Helen is more devoted to making love with Comrade José Morales than to working for party goals or being with Fisher. A competent painter, Fisher is weak of will and unreliable; he aspires to be a radical; he is not independent enough to follow his own beliefs. The people in Glen Cove apartments have better incomes than those in Twenty-Door City, but their personal lives symbolize the moral and social decay that has infected society. Mr. Franconi, the barber, has contracted venereal disease and commits suicide; the Russian couple, uncertain, suspicious, spy on each other; Mr. Boardman, salesman for marine engines, his daughter

away at school, frets over a mistress who double-crosses him; he loses
his life in the fire at the tenement house, where he has rented a room
from which to spy on his own apartment.

Not all losses spring from personal weakness or miscalculation;
some come from economic injustice and are impersonal, like fate. In a
warehouse on Lafayette Street, Old Running Water concludes that
someone must be fired when work slacks off after Christmas. Remembering that Hank Austin, a man given to making quips, "was absent
once about six months ago," he makes his decision; after Austin's
name, the Big Chief makes a dot as "large and black as a good-sized
bullet hole" (105). Without quite understanding why, Austin sees his
job slip away. He has little capacity to analyze or reflect. He believes
in President Hoover and in labor unions; he dislikes the "commoo-
nists" because they are foreigners, meaning Italians, believing that
they should all "go back where they came from" (131). He knows as
little about America as about Russia. Not given to thinking, he simply
believes. His chance participation in the big riot in Union Square and
the permanent injury that he receives make him a casualty of the kind
of economic warfare that defeated many, but left the future intact.

Man's determination to shape his future seems more certain than
the outcome. The big Red demonstration begins with a march and a
harangue, turns into a hum and a rumble, and ends with a rush of
action, as the rioting mob, creating itself, destroys with the same
senseless force that fire guts the tenement house. But as fire destroys,
so the gentle snow, soft and moist, cleanses and nourishes the changing landscape of Union Square:

the cops were busy knocking down the temporary speakers' plat-
forms. . . . Women and children stood by, waiting for the kindling
wood. . . .
    Toward the left, George Washington's powerful charger, facing due north,
did not bat an eyelash . . . (374–75).

But "The Man Who Walks Backwards," the man who faces the past,
yet hastens toward the future, clearly sees that "progress overleaps all
barriers. Time does not stop, it moves" (378). As the insatiable rain of
springtime washes away the winter slush, a "hard cold wind" whips
the pavement. The day awakens to new life, to the "tramp, tramp,
tramp, past Union Square," to a changing future that during the
1930's was, for all the agony and the losses, a time of hope, even joy.

III   *Reaction to* Union Square

Contemporary reaction to *Union Square*, an important part of the history of this novel, tells as much about the critical thinking of the era as it does about the specific novel. By the mid-1930's, the rather deep schism that had existed between the political and more aesthetic wings of radical thinking during the 1920's had, with the worsening economic conditions, given the political and social critics a new hearing. Now, any piece of writing, but especially one written with a social bias, was apt to be judged in terms of the new prescriptions that radical thinkers and partisan critics employed. Established reviewers continued to use their more disinterested approach or personal bias, but a novel that dealt with social problems was immediately thought of as "new writing."

Immediate reaction to *Union Square* was generally enthusiastic; the newspaper reviews, encouraging; the coverage, ample. William Soskin in the New York *Evening Post* called it an authentic picture of "the other half," and he praised the author for communicating "his warm, pitying sympathy to us as well as his sometimes contemptuous, sometimes kindly irony." [11] Soskin thought the story more readable than much of the recent work of Sinclair Lewis and John Dos Passos. In *The New York Times Book Review* John Chamberlain called Halper a "proletarian" writer, which meant that he "knows how to portray what happens to people when they are cast aside by a badly functioning economic system." In praising Halper's use of language, Chamberlain linked him to the tradition of Mark Twain and Ring Lardner. [12] The Boston *Evening Transcript* pointed to Halper's objectivity: "he ridicules Communism as much as he does the capitalists, and the proletariat as much as the police." But the reviewer thought the novel remained "a dreary picture and one that may appeal to those who care for what is morbid or weird." [13]

The Literary Guild, as it did with all of its selections, gave it special treatment. Writing a sensible and balanced evaluation for the Guild's promotional magazine *Wings*, Carl Van Doren admitted that *Union Square* would be classified as a proletarian novel, but insisted that it was "simply a book about unprivileged people who feel oppressed and who lay plans, most of them sporadic, for revolution." He thought the novel "something new in American literature," rich in raw materials and skillful in dramatization. The novel gave expression to communistic ideas, but it also offered a "great deal of intelligent criticism" of those ideas.[14]

The liberal weeklies, but especially the left-wing press, found the novel objectionable. Isidor Schneider thought Halper could "fit a story together," but had not produced a "first-class proletarian novel." The writer, he said, expressed little love for his characters; his emphasis was not on the suffering masses, but on sex.[15] Robert Cantwell found "no form underlying the confusion; the catastrophes are the results of accidents and coincidences; everything moves in a circle." [16] The most derogatory review came from Michael Gold in *New Masses*. Gold attacked the novel, the author, even the critics who had praised it. As he rightly said, the novel was clearly not "proletarian"; he thought it ought to have been. It was filled with misconceptions, he said, and contained not "one bitter cry of rage against capitalism." The stock characters had come from a "stale Bohemianism," which its author mistook for "social revolution." The whole book was synthetic, written by one with "no real social passions." The novel presented no real worker, not a person who suffers as the masses suffer today. Worse than all of these shortcomings, he concluded, the novel was "praised by the Van Dorens." [17]

What Halper had once said about faddism and the creative artist was equally true of the critic. In evaluating *Union Square*, critics did more than acknowledge new directions in the creative arts; they insisted on dictating the ideas that a writer must choose to express.

Partly because of its wide circulation and the controversy it generated, *Union Square* became Halper's best-known novel. It penetrated behind the facade of American urban life into the sickness and frustration of the personal lives of people at a time when revolutionary voices were seeking new ways to solve old problems. Events of the early 1930's seemed to confirm the truth that man's life was haunted by poverty and greed and despair in a land of plenty. To that complex scene of paradoxical attitudes and confusing personal allegiances, Halper gives order and control; the novel gains in unity and emotional impact as innocent and helpless men and women are ridden down and clubbed by the police in the pretense of preserving the law and furthering peace. Much of the novel's strength lies in its historical significance.

Union Square is a novel of idea, not of character. Clearly presented with humor and understanding, the characters are seldom motivated by inner conviction or compelling desire. Some, like Jason Wheeler and James Nicholson, possess intellect and self-assurance, but their achievements have been dissipated through losses and defeats. In Wheeler and Leon Fisher, the novel may have two heroes or no hero. Like the rest of the characters, their major part in the story seems only a minor act in the larger "revue" of historical and social happenings. They enact their roles, say their lines, move in and out of scenes, but the vitality and meaning of the roles they play derive from events; events impel them to act; events consume their lives. Their eternal mobility might have yielded growth and change, but it does not. The event forces Wheeler to speak; events elicit sympathy for Hank Austin's loss of work, not for Hank Austin. Drifters, loners, salesmen, painters, freight-handlers, peddlers, barbers, artists, lovers—they are caught between the past and the future, and while each is accorded a hearing, they seem more like newly found acquaintances who have been carefully observed than the deeply felt friends and relatives of the stories about Chicago.

Although *Union Square* is the story of individuals, their collective story makes up the life of the Square, which dominates and transcends all of them. What gives the novel undeniable power is Halper's honest and truthful treatment of his vision of human experience as the conflict between individuals and the changing ideas that confront them daily. He saw that man, in spite of dreams and hopes for a better life, had become little more than an automaton in a wasteland world; here, with his fears and desires, with his frustration and losses, man must cope with the collective strength and power that the Square symbolizes. The Square becomes, then, the battle ground of conflicting ideas, where man faces impersonal and unfathomable forces that erupt without sense or reason into violence and pain and death.

The structure of the novel moves in a circular pattern, turning on a hub of fate like the everlasting seasons that mark the change and progress of recorded time. *Union Square* ends, not with a solution, but with an ancient warning: everything that lives must change. As Halper writes, "progress overleaps all barriers. . . . For the future must be faced, no getting away from that . . ." (378). Through the power and certainty of change, the Square rules supreme. As individuals move into it, merge with the crowd, exert will and authority, the Square contains and creates and consumes. From it comes hope for man's best achievement, despair for his violent and corrosive struggle to survive.

In presenting his vision of modern urban and industrial America, Halper spoke directly to people in the depression-ridden 1930's. As a bit of history effectively written in strong and simple prose, *Union Square* reads like a well-organized intellectual exercise that has been based on vivid and recent observation. Halper's next four novels, all of them concerned with life in Chicago, show his developing strength as a novelist, for he writes them with the sensitivity and insight of deeply felt and long remembered experience.

CHAPTER 4

Remembering Chicago: Part I

"A young writer's life really begins when he leaves home," Halper said in *Good-bye, Union Square*.[1] New York was, he thought, the only other city worth acknowledging. In leaving Chicago he did not mean that he was seeking new material, although, as it happened, he was absorbing new experiences so that eventually New York furnished material for his first published novel. But the leaving and the distance had given a new perspective, had impelled him to look carefully at his own past. He had not lost actual contact with it; members of his family still lived in Chicago; he visited them and saw again the old places that he had known. Leaving Chicago had simply released a young writer's remembrances of the very city that he had left behind; these recollections came to dominate his writings for the next decade—and even longer.

Looking back on Chicago, he began to see it with a special pride and a feeling of compassion. "Chicago," he wrote in 1952, "has never been, nor tried to be, a city like New York, London, or Paris. It has always been, loudly and vociferously, itself."[2] He knew that many of the stories written about Chicago—some of them by non-Chicago writers—had cataloged the off-color spots or recorded the crimes and doings of the rich. Few writers had really probed into the city's interior or had seen behind the facade of juke boxes, beer joints, the "smiling women" who parade for conventioneers. As he believed, other stories were waiting to be written, stories of the thousands of people who were working and worrying and trying to adjust their lives to a new and changing world. Behind that "gigantic paper billboard" of a facade lay the real city, very much alive and breathing, with "a subtle inner complexity" that usually escaped the eye of the visitor.

To know that inner complexity, Halper thought, did not imply that a writer must have been born there. It did mean that a writer had to be "open-eyed and open-hearted," that he had walked the "grasses of Chicago's parks," visited in homes and grocery stores, watched the

workers going home at dusk and mingled with youthful crowds in the
ballrooms and bowling alleys, seen the ore-boats on Lake Michigan,
heard the printing presses, stared at the red glow of mills against the
sky, known the change of seasons in the city's parks, watched
"thousands of skaters" circling on the ice on a winter's Sunday afternoon.

But he thought that knowing Chicago had even greater significance. To know the events of the city and its inner history was to know
something of the "past and present of the country as a whole." As he
said, "Chicago was indeed America—only more so." To tell the story
of the city's inner life, then, was to tell the story of all America.
Halper's novels and stories, especially those about Chicago, seek to
reveal that "subtle inner complexity" of cities everywhere.

I   On the Shore

The success of *Union Square* prompted The Viking Press to bring
out a collection of Halper's short stories, most of them about growing
up in Chicago and all of them about his own experiences. Of the
fifteen, all except one, "A Parting in the Country," had been published in magazines. The opportunity gave him the chance to select
and republish the best stories in book form and thus make them more
readily available. Since all of the stories have a common narrator and
many of them deal with the same related characters, Halper suggested that the volume be designated a novel or even an autobiography, although it is strictly neither. He gave the stories continuity by
organizing them into three sections that show the narrator's growth.
In the first story he is five years old; in the final story he has reached
maturity and is remembering his past and sometimes the present as
he writes these pieces in a far distant city. *On the Shore*, subtitled
Young Writer Remembering Chicago was published in February,
1934.

The stories in *On the Shore* seem quaintly pastoral, like an old
photograph album of family scenes and visiting relatives. As remembrances of life on Chicago's West Side, they have the authenticity of
personal history, and in developing the idea of the narrator's growth,
Halper shows the boy's expanding consciousness as he absorbs the
life of the family and works in his father's grocery store, enters a larger
world of adolescence and young manhood and, finally, the world of
work, where his men and women struggle with the pain and laughter
of life. Loosely sequential like those of Joyce's *Dubliners* or Ander-

son's *Winesburg, Ohio*, the collected stories gain depth and breadth
with Halper's arrangement: each story gives a kind of continuity and a
developing reenforcement to the other. The memories belong to the
narrator Dave, who tells of the quirks and foibles of his own family,
but his memories also reflect the inner feelings and complexity of his
city and its people.

The initial story in *On the Shore*, "A Herring for My Uncle,"
describes a journey into the family's past. The letter that arrives from
an uncle in New Zealand prompts a visit to Uncle Gustav, who came
to Chicago long ago with his shrewish wife. He has had many jobs,
including his present one in a cigar factory. Uncle Gustav's life has
been one of losses—he had been tricked into marriage, had given up
his hope of becoming a scholar. Now he is ill with fatigue and fits of
coughing. The herring that the narrator takes as a gift serves as a bond
of memory that reveals the feelings and emotion of many immigrants
who worked and struggled and sometimes survived and often lost.
The small joy that the offering brings is part of the social history of an
era.

"My Aunt Daisy," one of Halper's best and best known, portrays
the theme of loneliness, a motif that is repeated in the novels and in
many stories. The maiden aunt from Boston with vivacious manners
and Eastern ways has come to Chicago for a visit. Although growing
old, she still has hopes. She meets and falls in love with Harry
O'Callahan, a young railroader, who sings ballads and pitches
horseshoes. When young Harry ruptures himself by hoisting pails of
sand, Aunt Daisy retreats to tears and to the loneliness that awareness
of her losses brings. Without money, she must beg the return fare to
Boston from the narrator's father; she has lost her pride, her little
security of manners and customs; her loneliness turns into enmity.

The early stories, almost wholly family centered, give way to the
narrator's adventures and exploits in the "outside" world. Curious
and adventuresome, the narrator asserts his independence. He dives
for pennies in the park and loses; he fails to win an ice-skating race.
On a trip to the fruit market with his father, he witnesses a Negro
being knifed by two white truckers. Although the problems, the
moods, the inner feelings in the process of growing up are much
the same anywhere, the environment was not quite the same as the
woods and lakes of Michigan that Hemingway knew or the Winesburg, Ohio, of Sherwood Anderson.

In part Three, the losses and regrets of youth are displaced by
lessons of guilt and death, of man and the machine, by lessons in

forbearance and courage that any young artist needs to know if he is trying to understand the human condition. In "Farm Hand" a boy visiting the city—and clearly from the country—runs into the grocery store, seeking help. He has just been assaulted by Pickles, a young hoodlum whom even the narrator knows about. "I felt it was my duty to help this fellow," Dave argues with himself, "but my common sense told me I couldn't do it. If I helped him, Pickles would have something on me." [3] Although the farm boy evades his assailant by jumping a streetcar, Dave wrestles with his guilt. In frustration, he beats up his younger brother for staying away from the store so long.

In "My Mother's Uncle from Lithuania," the death of the narrator's mother brings an end to family solidarity; ". . . a week later we moved into a smaller flat in another section of the city; and soon after that the family broke up" (161). "On the Shore," which furnishes the title for the volume, "The Feud in the Rotunda," and "White Laughter" describe the narrator's job experiences in the post office, his growing awareness of the feud between man and the machine, his deep and thoughtful laughter as he remembers the people from his past on a snowy night in New York. As he thinks of his Indian friend at the post office (see Chapter 2) telling about gods and standing strong and talking straight amidst all the confusion, he too feels the strength of the "big white flakes of snow," that, falling strong and straight, merge into "one strength" within himself. "I felt myself standing steady as a great rock while the snow kept falling" (208). This acquired feeling of "strength" impels a laughter that reveals his capacity both to understand and to grow.

Although most of the stories are concerned with the relation of the writer to the outside world and with the doings of others, "Young Writer Remembering Chicago" (already discussed in Chapter 2) focuses primarily on the writer's inner life. Revised only slightly from earlier versions, it remains highly impressionistic in thought and technique, a stream of memories, a recollection of sights and sounds which have given thought and meaning to the author's early life and afforded keen insights into the inner life of the city.

None of the stories strives to make formal resolution of problems and dilemmas that happen to people everywhere. But in "My Brothers Who Are Honest Men," the final story of the collection, (see Chapter 2) the insistence on the values of honesty, integrity, and sincerity may constitute Halper's program for action. Such values apply equally to individuals of any race or creed and to all groups, whatever the organized prejudices, the political aims and sympathies.

Critical reaction to *On the Shore* varied. Harold Strauss thought the sketches "diffuse and repetitive," simply "autobiographical ramblings" that any writer might wish to set down and forget.[4] Alvah Bessie, recognizing the authenticity of the "deeply-felt, personal experience," thought the stories were really "impotent fumbling with the manifestations of emotion," not an elucidation of it. They were written, he said, in the "flat, monotonous prose that Sherwood Anderson inaugurated."[5] The *New Republic* thought the stories "simply, firmly and effectively done," but with a "certain laziness of style."[6] Almost alone of all the critics, Horace Gregory saw that the volume had form and pattern and that it transcended the "usual human document" to reach into the great city beyond.[7]

The left-wing press was satisfied with neither Halper's technique nor his political thinking. Writing in the *Daily Worker*, Wallace Phelps declared that the stories were disappointing, not because Halper couldn't write, but because there was too much of the young writer remembering and not "enough of the social perspective which Halper must have arrived at by now." In short, Halper had used too much psychology and not enough party line. As Phelps said, "since Halper is personally sympathetic to the revolutionary movement, it was expected that he would bite deeper into its core. . . ."[8]

Norman Macleod continued the exhortation in *New Masses*. *On the Shore*, he thought, was "more substantially real" than *Union Square*; Halper was "sincere and honest and struggling," but he had problems that needed to be corrected. ". . . he tries to be too objective and detached. He relies upon emphasis rather than bias. And this is wrong. Every writer should have a bias. We can only hope that his bias may become Communist. For his own good and ours."[9] Although the Communists failed to win him to their point of view or persuade him to join the Party, he became involved with them during the summer of 1934 in a literary squabble over definition and critical terminology.

II *What is Proletarian Writing?*

"I don't know what proletarian writing is," Halper told his agent Max Lieber. Lieber, a Communist Party member, thought Halper was joking. He was not. Nor was he uninformed. He knew the literary trends of the era; he knew the people that had become literary material. He had grown up with workers, had been one himself. He knew their needs and problems, but when he wrote about them, he saw them as individuals, as people he had known in one way or another. He did not write about the struggling masses for the same reason that he did not write about rich people. He had never known any. He had written about strikes and riots and political argument in *Union Square* because he had witnessed these events and had listened to people argue the issues. He rebelled against labels, especially literary labels such as "proletarian writer," with its "cheap, easy connotations" and its doubtless "fleeting and dubious vogue." [10]

During the 1930's the term had acquired a variety of meanings. Floyd Dell may have invented the phrase as early as 1919 when he referred to the "Proletarian Novel of Revolt" in one of his book reviews. [11] Young activists of the 1920's and early '30's like Michael Gold, Joseph Freeman, and V. F. Calverton, had given the term currency. They had linked it with radical contemporary writing that followed socialist thinking and Marxian or Communist ideology. By whatever process, the meaning of the term had broadened to include writing that dealt with the urban poor, the workers in mills and factories, the unemployed, the transient and homeless, and so on. Any writing that described the downtrodden as well as the down and out invited an application of the term. That reviewers and critics should fasten it to Halper's writing was, of course, inevitable; he was indeed dealing with social issues and workers and human problems in the world of the '30's, but he was writing neither social propaganda nor political persuasion.

He had not, however, insulated himself from the contemporary world. As he said,

. . . the Depression, somehow, was my time. Deny it or not, it was coloring my writing strongly. Though irritation and anger often gripped me as shallow and frequently dishonest pronouncements emanated from the left, theirs was the prime potent voice raised during the thirties. [12]

His refusal to join the Party had not endeared him to members and fellow travelers, but he had not militated against them in any offensive way. Actually, in an open letter to *New Masses* in February, 1934, he praised the magazine for its "revolutionary program" as "the only way out of the mess and wreckage which our statesmen still insist on calling civilization." He said that he endorsed their "editorial policy" and that he would be glad to send them "material in the future." [13] He was surprised, though, to see his story about a slum school in Chicago—"A Morning with the Doc"—in the magazine's May issue; his agent had sent it without consulting him. Later, his essay, "The Plight of the Postal Subs," appeared in the July issue. A

change in *New Masses* policy had already begun to appear long before
the Seventh World Congress of the Communist International met in
August, 1935, and inaugurated the Popular Front, which enabled a
person to support the Communist Party and Franklin D. Roosevelt,
labor, the middle classes, and the Negro all at the same time.[14] *New
Masses* began publishing such non-Communist writers as Thomas
Mann, Sherwood Anderson, Ernest Hemingway, and many others
including Halper.

In the summer of 1934, Halper became further embroiled with
Party argument. When Sender Garlin asked him to contribute to
Garlin's "Change the World!" column in the *Daily Worker*, Halper
accepted. In a long letter-essay, he sharply criticized Marxian critics
for being "intellectually lazy." Three groups, he thought, constituted
the present literary scene: the genteel writers, the "grim faced"
proletarian, and the "confused" ones or "fence sitters," who, he said,
possess the most talent and "are hard-working as well as honest."
Good critics, said Halper, are like "shock troops." "They always
precede good novelists. They level the ground, they clear the stumps
away. . . . Mencken, though he was never a left-winger, was the last
of the old war-horses. Under his drive we have gotten the best out of
Dreiser, Lewis and others." Halper predicted that of the "dozen real
novelists" on the scene, few would become major writers because
they will have to do "too much pioneer work." [15] Halper's letter
accomplished two things: it declared his own position of independence; it demanded an answer from the left-wing press. Joseph
Freeman responded.

In his long article "Ivory Towers—White and Red," Freeman
admitted that Marxian critics had yet to solve the crucial problem of
criticism, but that Halper's formulation of the problem was wrong.
Halper, he said, "shows no awareness of the dynamics of our literary
movement as it has developed in the past ten years." [16] The fact is,
Freeman said, that Marxians have not had a chance to develop
criticism; they have failed to publish "fundamental works," but that
failure was now being corrected. As early as 1932, he said that he had
himself submitted to the John Reed Club a proposed list of critical
books and pamphlets to be written by various writers of the left. An
even more fundamental change, he admitted, had been taking place
in the thinking of the organization—the sectarian attitude of the Party
was being abandoned. As late as 1933, Freeman said,

The "line" was jealously guarded. Now the opposite is true. Anyone has only
to declare himself a "fence-sitter" and he is embraced with open arms; our

press is his and he can say anything he likes, however remote it may be from revolutionary thought.[17]

The "old ivory towers are down" and "so are the red ivory towers which sectarianism built." [18]

What had redirected the American intelligentsia, Freeman continued, was the fact that the "crisis has cut the ground from under the feet of the middle-class and its intellectual sons and daughters." [19] With an increase in the number of people fighting on the "cultural front" of Communism, writers will now have more time to devote to criticism. Actually, neither a change in Communist policy nor a concern for criticism had altered Halper's direction, but reviews of his work in *New Masses* had already grown more appreciative.

Ironically, the magazine's scolding had been mostly correct. He had never had their bias nor did he swing closer to it. Perhaps Leslie Fiedler is right in saying that comrades in America, including fellow travelers, lived mostly in "the half-invented world of the party press" and judged themselves "by its editorials rather than by the reactions of their neighbors." [20] The world in which Halper lived had always been the real world of experience; as he said later, he thought some people needed the Party to fulfill themselves. He did not.

I was sympathetic to some of its aims, as were many non-Party intellectuals, but these broad aims, I knew, were not the exclusive property of any political organization—anyone could be in favor of them—and consequently I didn't feel any sense of loyalty to the Party line.[21]

Certainly he had never needed any party to inform him of economic problems or human needs. The evidence lay all around him—the ever-present bread lines, the meagre faces of the unemployed were visible and painful reminders of the need for social solutions. No sensitive person needed a lecturer from Webster Hall to tell him that times were difficult.

Yet, personally, he was better off than ever. With good sales from *Union Square* and *On the Shore*, he "was moderately affluent." He bought a few clothes and even began stopping at art galleries as his interest in art revived. And very soon he started work on a new novel, this time about his work experience in a Chicago electrotype foundry. He began making notes and tentative outlines; whole scenes and "pages of dialogue flashed" into his mind. As he said, "I hungered to cram all the characters I'd known in that foundry into colorful solid scenes." He recalled the arguments of the molders; the breakdown of the new labor saving machine; the suicide in the company toilet; the three bosses, who fought among themselves; the one-eyed caster who visited the lady barbers every Saturday. "It was," he said, "the usual time of frenzy every novelist goes through before the actual period of writing begins." [22]

By mid-November, 1933, a first draft had run to almost 150,000 words. He felt that he had written with "as much economy as I can command," but he also knew that he would have to revise and rework some of the material. Still the writing had gone well; in certain parts he thought that he had "finally found myself." [23] By mid-February, 1932, a revised draft still seemed "too heavy and slow"; he worked constantly, trying "to prune and snap the stuff up." [24] By July he was checking the galleys with great care, noting the changes that his editor, David Zablodowky, had made on the galley sheets, and not always agreeing with him. Actually, he restored some of the changes—he wanted lump, not limp; grittled, not gritted; churned, not drove. "These are juicy words," he told Zablodowsky, "and even if they are not quite kosher they sound better, to me, than the ones you suggested." He wanted other restorations. Evidently Zablodowsky had been bothered by Halper's "habit of repetition." "These repetitions," Halper wrote, "are studied and spotted to the best of my ability and, frankly, I like 'em. . . . Also, I displace an adjective occasionally, if I feel it will enhance the rhythm of a sentence." [25] What the reviewers and readers called sloppy and careless use of language was, whatever the inaccuracy, intentional with Halper. He was simply taking a calculated risk in saying it his own way. *The Foundry* appeared in September, 1934.

III The Foundry

In *Union Square* Halper had described the contemporary scene in New York. In the next four novels, he writes about Chicago, giving shape and structure to past experiences with a slangy vitality of thought and feeling that adds sinew and individuality to his style and content. *The Foundry*, first of the Chicago novels, employs many of the same techniques as *Union Square*—a collective symbol as hero, a broad canvas of characters, historical events as shaping factors in the lives of individuals, a structuring of events that relates the lives of the characters to the natural world. Halper laces his clear and simple prose with flashes of poetry, insight, and humor. Although *The Foundry* is partly a study of the growing power of labor unions at the time of the 1929 crash, it is primarily an examination of the complex problem that has been developing since the eighteenth century: the relation of man to the machine.

As Halper says, *The Foundry* is the story of "a few characters, streets, buildings, and pieces of machinery, not to mention the hum that the dynamos make when the current is turned on full force in the foundry." [26] As a collectivity, the foundry includes the place as well as the people, the tools of production as well as energy and power. As container and shaper of individual thought and action, the foundry is a kind of collective hero that is both agency and agent. An ever-present idea and force in the lives of the characters, it unites them in purpose, separates them with antagonisms, consumes and destroys, shelters and protects. This "place where printing plates are made," this "roaring, crashing jungle of men and machines and hammering noise" is a microcosm of industrial life, which operates on the ethics of hard work and the shaping specter of fear. From eight to five, the place is a bedlam of hate and horror, of deafening noise, a square cave with wheels and gears, a fateful mechanical world that has been wrought by the machine.

Machinery dominates. It creates a darksome and suspicious world that matches the dark and windy weather of the autumnal gloom. The printeries stretch "like a row of barracks." Huge locomotives give forth a "mournful chugging." Smoke hangs in the air. The wind grows raw and damp. Man, like a pencil dot, pressed and squeezed on sidewalk and trolley, has been caught in the trap of his own inventions. The will of man, with which he tries to shape the individual and collective worlds, proves ineffectual against the fateful frustrations and hapless harmony of the collective force of the foundry. Although the labor union serves as a strong counter force against the owners, the resolution of the problems comes, not from the triumph of union policy and action, but from the individual worker's momentary insight into the mystical and harmonious nature of his own job. But brief insight neither abolishes a world of losses and defeats nor redeems it.

In the foundry—as in the world of the machine—time is the common denominator that all but determines man's way of life. Time accounts for the precision of the machine, the daily routine, the dead line. It determines monotony, sameness, frustration, submission. It equals money, profit, the hourly wage, overtime, the possible road to paradise for the down and out. Although the clock measures time, so do the seasons—the wind of winter, the "twitterings" of spring. As man's moods are created, so time dictates and determines his inner world of thought and feeling. Time is even more basic and universal; it is the rhythm of man's heart beat, the stuff of life, the sound and rhythm of song and laughter.

As in *Union Square*, Halper uses seasonal change to structure events of the novel, and these events, both public and private, merge to form the inner "weather," the feelings, the thoughts and disposition of the characters. Parts One and Two—the autumn of 1928—introduce and portray mostly external aspects of the Fort Dearborn Electro-type Foundry, the three owners, "the foundry men and their brides, the machines," but there are also glimpses of their little private worlds of sickness and dreams, of regrets and frustrations, of brutalities and sympathies. The three partners, squabbling and untrustworthy, are a tyrannical trio of ex-foundry workers, who have risen to positions of management. Ezekiel Cranly, senior member of the firm, formerly bookkeeper at the foundry, suffers from hemorrhoids, is weak and ineffectual, openly hated by the junior partner, Mr. Jack Duffy, who, brash and wise-cracking, earns the contempt of the other partners and the patient tolerance of the workers. The real boss, Max'l Steuben, with his bright blue pig-like eyes in a mountain of flesh, tyrannizes both partners. He dreams of his inventions, asserts his authority with an unpredictable personal bias. No agent of common sense, Max'l storms and blusters with the force of expedient action.

Much of foundry life is revealed through the eyes and experiences of a newcomer, August Kafka, who, as he learns the job of shipping clerk, introduces the reader, who likewise is a newcomer, to the office and shop, to the jobs and machines, to the sights and sounds of industrial life and, finally, to Kafka's private world of music. He has grown up on Chicago's West Side; he is used to working, but the noise is another thing. When he ascends the rat-trap elevator to the top floor of the foundry, he believes that he has stepped into a madhouse. From behind the partition of the clerk's office, "the pneumatic hammers, the saws, and other machinery were making a terrific racket" (13). The telephone rattles away. The human voice competes to be heard and mostly loses. Only Max'l is comforted by the noise. He comes in the office like a tornado. His stare "flew past the new shipping clerk, took note of Miss Weber in the inner doorway, went winging past Jack Duffy, and, like an arrow, sped straight and true between the senior partner's shoulder blades" (15). Like a cool wind, the machinery soothes and sustains his growing awareness of a serious heart condition. Everywhere life has become a matter of fragments, pieces of isolation, scraps of loneliness.

In part Three, "When winter comes to Chicago," there is a turning inward, a concern for personal problems, a probing "deeper into the bosoms of the boys," into their hopes, fears, their little animosities and private gripes, into the petty bickering among the three partners. At home Duffy slips out on his wife to meet Mrs. Hill. The other two partners, Max'l and Cranly, invest in stocks that fail to advance. In the office, Miss Weber is hounded by Saul Epstein, who comes for an order, but follows her out to lunch. Even the Christmas cigar list causes argument. Labor trouble develops, coming as much from stubborn pride and personal vindictiveness as from theoretical conviction or reforming zeal. Actually Old Max'l has hired Karl Heitman, "the most radical electrotyper in the city," out of sheer bravado. Heitman begins talking to the men, urges them "to start thinking and tracing things to their sources" (196). He tells them about economics and philosophy; he talks to them in terms of "good old common horse sense" (136). They listen to his abstract explanations, but they act in terms of personal gain, individual relationships, private concerns. They delight in making the place around the sink wet and sloppy in the hopes that Max'l will slip and fall.

The explosive actions in the plant are caused by a collision of individual temperaments as much as from the antagonism of management and labor. Trouble comes when the workers break their own union rules. Slavony, one of the tank men, eats his lunch on company time. He is immediately fired. Although he is entirely at fault, the men take his side; they retaliate against Max'l by a work slow-down and by sending through blotched plates. Tension mounts. Each side engages in game-playing, plotting strategies and biding for power. Any act is an issue—the workers quibble over the new office furniture as unnecessary expense. The three partners somehow realize that the change of a desk or chair will not solve the deeper problems of self.

As their industrial warfare increases and both sides undermine the process on which both sides depend, so individuals gain and lose. In the past the grim business of work has exalted man's pride, justified a certain submission, clarified a need for the mastery of craft, a domination of the machine. To a new generation of workers, success meant sabotaging the process if necessary, changing the procedure to fit a purpose, ruining plates to achieve control, accepting "trouble" as part of the business of working and, perhaps, as the only way of exalting human values and fulfilling human needs. Their concerted

effort in doing sloppy work constitutes man's revenge, not against the
machine, but against the injustice of man and his unwise use of
power.

Only when Slavony is rehired do the men settle down to business.
Private concerns remain paramount. Buckley advertises for a widow
who is interested in an affair. Mr. Cranly attends to his piles. Old
Max'l suffers a heart attack. Slavony's baby dies. Cassius Hurowski's
son is arrested. Both for bosses and workers, the winter has brought
sickness and despair, a subtle corroding from within. Down the street
Chin Moy's restaurant is held up. At the hospital four foundlings are
left on the door step. Yet, even as the cold strengthens, so the January
thaw comes on schedule. As young Kafka stares at the snow sweeping
across the tower of the rail station, his foot begins to tap out the
rhythm of a medley of foundry sounds.

With the coming of spring in part Four, there is a momentary
revival of spirit, a turning outward. "The windows up and down the
streets of the printing trades began to open one by one" (234). Kubec
moves to the country to avoid high rents; Pete, the caster, visits the
back room in the ladies' barbershop—for a manicure; Old Hooper-
Dooper is caught imitating Max'l's walk; he is summarily dismissed.
As the wind blows warm and the sun blazes down, the city seems
drunk with spring. "I didn't sleep so good last night, men," quips
Pinky. "I was tossing about until the aurora borealis faded, boys"
(262).

Summer brings a rash of accidents, a falling apart of body and spirit.
Knetski is caught by the cylinder teeth of his hacker because he has
failed to flip back the handle quickly enough. Old Bunsen Burner,
concealing the pain from his hernia, returns to the finishing table and
tries to keep working. Franck, the wax-caster, loses his grip on
reality; when old Max'l urges him to work a little faster, he pulls a
knife on the boss. Two policemen are needed to haul him away.

The miracle of man's inventiveness creates an insoluble problem.
Max'l's new machine can complete the whole process of finishing the
plates in a single operation, thus eliminating the jobs of three or four
men. For him the invention represents the creative product of his
engineering mind; his effort has come as inevitable as change. In
building and exhibiting the new machine, he has as much honest
pride in his achievement as any worker. Yet, as the labor agent points
out, "Laying off three or four men who have families on their hands is
a serious business" (325). Concepts of progress and humanity, even
when supported by statistics, remain undefined, downright mystical.

When convenient, both labor and management retreat to their hierarchical ideals, which protect the status quo as if in some medieval relationship. Often under the same label, man treats and mistreats his fellow creatures. Lacking a capacity to fulfill the expectations and ideals that he can readily conceive, he alienates and destroys both himself and others. Lacking a needed wisdom, he seeks for answers in new fads and new follies. "Don't think we can keep on beating the machines forever . . . ," Karl Heitman warns the workers. With the end of summer comes a turning, a ripeness, the end of a season, the end of an era.

In part Five, the wind, rain, and foggy evenings of autumn in 1929 portend "that this fall was to be slightly different." As the economy ripens in the "golden financial sunshine," an ominous and vague future casts its shadow of economic despair: "In the east a handful of small stubborn clouds lay low and threatening against the financial skyline" (378). Man, even the captains of industry, the heads of great banking houses, the officials of the federal government, cannot prevent or stop the decay that appears everywhere.

Foundry conditions are chaotic. Old Zeke has forgotten to mark a rush order; the local crime wave reaches into the foundry office with the robbery of the payroll; Kubec, in pursuit of his wife's lover, threatens to burn him with kerosene; junior partner Duffy, trapped by his adulterous escapades, takes to drink; worry over the wavering stock market has shaken the security of the partners. Karl Heitman's harangues on the cunningness of employers sounds harshly ironic—as the facts would have it, one has committed suicide; another has suffered a heart attack; a third, "stricken with piles, also lay home in bed, tossing feverishly and shouting something in a half-shriek about the stock market" (481). For the individual, whether he is worker or boss, whether for or against the social body, the question remains: is the cure simply a matter of economics?

If a unique strength lies with the collectivity, that strength is achieved, not by diagnosis of the profit motive or by the propaganda of union radicals, but by a unity of vision that reaches the individual through art. What unites the workers is August Kafka's musical composition, *The Printing House Blues*. When the workers recognize that "the violins rising to a high, ungodly pitch" is the "screaming of the hydraulic presses," they become "for the first time in their lives . . . fully conscious of the song of their own machines" (476). Their recognition of a relation to the machine is vision more mystical than Marxian. As Halper writes,

The foundrymen, listening, sat electrified in their seats. Their throats, filled with the dumb thick wonder of their labor, began to expand, shouting voicelessly. Their heads began to perspire, to burst. . . . Good Lord, what were they listening to! They were listening to the song of their own machines! For the first time in their lives they began to realize that something—something— (477)

The "dumb thick wonder" that the music reveals to them is the unheard melody that brings the voiceless shout, the sudden insight into the nature of their work. Their response to the music enables them to glimpse the wonder of an integrated and harmonious world, to feel the deeper faith and the stronger hope. August Kafka—and Halper—have transformed the babble of industrial noise into a hymn of joy.

The Foundry ends, not with the symphonic hymn to the printing plant, but with Jack Duffy's suicide. The men are stunned into silence. Karl Heitman, who feels little pity for the man, reminds the workers that Duffy received two hundred dollars a week for standing around with a pencil over his ear, while a worker did the job and received only seventeen. Duffy's death causes little more than a brief interruption in the day's routine. The sabotage of the new machine, the strike, the death are but incidents in a long season of industrial development that bring few advances and little progress. Although Halper's criticism is not didactic, he is well aware of the problems. As novelist, his way is other—he writes of the effect of poverty on the workers, of their moral values, their treatment of each other, and of the power of the machine, which both enslaves and liberates.

The Foundry shows a marked advance over *Union Square*. In his second novel Halper is on home ground, speaking with the familiarity of long experience. Out of a knowledge that is intensive and precise, a memory that is remarkable for reconstructing detail, he creates character and scene with compassion and clarity. The novel abounds with sensory detail; as artist-historian he relies on sight and sound, describing at length, for example, the exact process used in making electroplates and in preparing them for shipment; or in the men's reaction to a new piece of machinery or a change in working conditions. The processes and the reactions become dramatic elements of the story.

He portrays his characters with the same objectivity, for their inner world of thought and feeling is conveyed through descriptions of what the narrator sees and hears, of what the character says and does; the foibles and mannerisms of behavior; the nature of a worker's specialized skill; his limitations and inability to achieve and grow. Whether as individuals or as individuals working together, nobody really wins. With a little guidance, they all stick together long enough to exact a revenge or to glimpse their part in August Kafka's musical composition. For a little while, the memory of that recognition of their own being lingers, then quickly fades with the increasing din of the machines. Only August Kafka has understood the agony of the experience well enough for him to capture it, as Halper has done, and for that memory to linger on as wisdom and wonder.

Ironical and broadly humorous, coarse in no offensive way, *The Foundry* is a carefully wrought novel, telling the story of both worker and "overseer," both labor and capital, a history of and a commentary on the impact and the process through which an industrial world molds and determines the pattern of human life.

IV *Contemporary Reaction to* The Foundry

The Foundry received a wider, but no better press than *Union Square* and *On the Shore*. In a front-page review in the Sunday *New York Herald Tribune Books*, Sinclair Lewis called the novel "earthy, solid, human, and decidedly significant—and what is far less to have been expected it is along with these grave qualities, also humorous and dramatic." The characters, he found, were real individuals, not simply "proletarian" types. The author, he said, "has something of the skill of a Mr. Dickens or a Mr. Turner in making beauty out of grime. . . ." Lewis thought Halper should be taken seriously along with Hemingway, Dos Passos, Faulkner, John O'Hara.[27]

Other reviewers qualified their praise. Peter Quennell thought the novel "much solider, better written" than *Union Square*; if the style "borrows something from James Joyce" and is never dull, the writing is "often ponderous, now and then a little turgid."[28] Lewis Gannett called Halper a "George Grosz" of the printed page, writing "a conglomerate of good short stories," rather "than a single well-knit novel."[29] James Burnham noted the novel's "vigor, its earthy breeziness, its accurate observation," but thought it without organic form and without fully developed characters, which were realized only as types, with odd and strained pecularities.[30] Alvah Bessie summarized the novel with a dismissal—the novel remains, he said, "amorphous, lumbering clumsily through chapter after chapter, in which nothing, literally, happens."[31]

The Communist press followed a familiar line. Joseph North praised Halper as a

first rate writing man. He can spin a yarn when he has a mind to: he can, more vividly than I have seen in any of our younger American writers, give the feel, the smell, the sound of our brick and electric jungles in which the industrial proletariat lives and dies. [32]

But the trouble, North said, was that Halper would not create strictly proletarian characters or go in the right "ideological direction." Politically, he was still a fence straddler. As a writer he introduced his characters like a "white, superior interlocutor . . . introducing the black-face characters." [33] Such condescension derives from "Menckenian corrosion"—"The late Mencken gave Halper his first break and made made him pay dearly for the privilege. He transmitted to Halper delusions of grandeur." The result is "snootiness." Besides, North explained, having been praised by the Literary Guild, the Van Dorens, and Sinclair Lewis, Halper had become little more than a "petty-bourgeois 'proletarian' writer." [34] If he is to become a "true artist," Halper must "go with the forces of creation" and join the one true Party. Although Joseph Freeman had reported that the Communists had abandoned their sectarian attitude, the missionary zeal of *New Masses* continued as petulant and biased as ever.

CHAPTER 5

Remembering Chicago: Part II
(The Chute)

"THE hot breath of radical culture was everywhere in the air,"
Halper said, speaking of 1935.[1] Roosevelt's election had
already restored a measure of national confidence. The bread lines,
the apple sellers, the "Hoovervilles" had decreased in number, but
had not completely disappeared. Panaceas for social and economic
betterment were coming from both the Right and the Left and from
any part of the country.

Near Detroit Father Charles E. Coughlin, turning against
Roosevelt in 1934, began his tirades against the Jews and Jewish
bankers. In California Dr. Francis E. Townsend proposed giving
$200 a month pension to every person over sixty years of age with the
stipulation that it had to be spent immediately. In Louisiana Senator
Huey Long fathered a plan of bringing economic health to the nation
under the slogan "Share Our Wealth Society—Every Man a King."
The Democrats inaugurated their own "New Deal" program. As the
government began passing new social and economic legislation, the
conclusion seemed inescapable that government believed itself to be
ultimately responsible for providing employment and for promoting
the security and welfare of all people.

With the continuing social and economic unrest, radical thinking
became more acceptable and more aggressive. Socialist and communist ideas began infiltrating the workers' unions and other political
action groups. Former Communists like Whittaker Chambers, whom
Halper had met once in New York and did not like, began finding
positions in the government in Washington. College students, mostly
from middle class homes, joined in marches and demonstrations and
began shouting slogans about strikes and the recognition of labor
unions.

Intellectuals, writers, poets, artists—many of them had now
turned their attention to those Americans who were ill-fed, ill-

housed, and ill-clothed and who made up, President Roosevelt said, "one-third of a nation." Exiles and expatriates, many who had left America in the 1920's, began trickling back from their long season in Paris and on the Riviera. Malcolm Cowley, one of them, concluded in 1934 that propaganda need not be all bad. Because artists "are men before they are writers or painters, and because their human interests are involved, and because they can't stay out of the battle without deliberately blinding and benumbing themselves," Cowley argued, they may very well take part in the class struggle. He hoped they would; "I hope and trust that a great number of them will take the workers' side, and I think that doing so will make them better artists." [2]

In April, 1935, at the First American Writers' Congress, which met in New York and was sponsored by the Communist Party, Hays Jones declared that the working class was the only live thing in this capitalist society. The man who "spends nine hours in front of a punch press or on a ship," he said, "has more reality, more beauty and more harmony than you will find in all of Park Avenue with its boredom, its waste of time and its quest for joy that doesn't exist." [3] With its emphasis on time and work, the communist prescription for artistic growth and social usefulness sounded as if it might have come from *Poor Richard's Almanack* as from the *Daily Worker*. Their slogans were sometimes only an old Puritanism writ new.

For the young writer remembering Chicago, the ubiquity of radical culture was his lucky break. He had perhaps been a worker first and then a writer; certainly he had been born at the right time. Because his beliefs had come to him, not from prescribed theory, but out of need and experience, he had maintained his independence and his objectivity. As a thinker and a writer, he saw the human condition with his own bias, however narrow and restricted it might prove to be. Speaking of the new writers of the 1930's such as Robert Cantwell, Albert Halper, James T. Farrell, Edward Dahlberg, Daniel Fuchs; Alfred Kazin has said, "the real excitement of the new period was in the explosion of personal liberation which such writers brought in from the slums, farms and factories. . . ." [4] Halper's own experience had given him first-hand insight into the problems and conditions of labor. *The Foundry* demonstrated his knowledge of factory life; his next novel offered a second excursion into the life of working class people and a look at one of America's unique institutions—the mail-order house.

I   *The Guggenheim Fellowship*

By the time *The Foundry* was published in the autumn of 1934, Halper had already sailed for England. At the suggestion of his friend Louis Adamic, he had applied for and received a Guggenheim Fellowship, with the stipulation that he spend the year in a foreign country. Leaving the last of August, he sailed for Southampton and eventually settled in North London near Hampstead, where, much as he had lived in New York, he did his own cooking and began work on a new novel. His friendship with Edward and Constance Garnett led in part to his trip to Russia.

The Garnetts were already well known in the literary world. Edward Garnett, a reader at Duckworth's, had befriended many writers, including John Galsworthy and Joseph Conrad. Constance Garnett had gained a reputation for translating Russian novelists and introducing them to the English speaking public. Halper shared this enthusiasm for Russian writers, and partly because of the Garnetts' urging and partly because *The Foundry* had been published in Russian translation and had accumulated royalties which he might reclaim, Halper journeyed to Moscow in April, 1935. Since the Soviet Union did not recognize American copyrights and would not send an author's royalties outside the country, he was thus able to collect some of the money that was rightfully his.

In Moscow he met a number of writers, including Walt Carmon, editor of the English edition of *International Literature*; Sergei Dinamov, head of the Russian Association of Proletarian Writers; Sergei Tretyakov, leader of the left Front and rival of Dinamov; and Bertolt Brecht, who had just escaped from Nazi Germany. He watched the big May Day celebration in Red Square with a Canadian girl, who had recognized him as an American and had spoken to him. The girl had given up her Canadian citizenship to remain in Moscow and work for the "revolutionary future of the world." Now she was trapped. Her plight horrified Halper. The brief description of his Russian visit that he wrote in *Good-bye, Union Square* thirty years later tells how a journey to the mecca of Communism failed to win him as a convert.

On his return to New York, he suddenly found himself a well-established writer, with more money than he had ever had before. *The Foundry* had already gone into several printings. Metro-Goldwyn-Mayer had bought the film rights, although the picture never reached the production stage. The trip to Russia had given him prestige with the left-wing press; the editor of *Soviet Russia Today* asked for articles; the *New Masses* editors urged him to make a lecture tour. In both instances he was, of course, expected to subscribe to the party line, which he refused to do. Instead, he worked on his own, finished a few short stories and the novel he had begun in England, and started writing another. *The Chute*, the second published novel about Chicago, appeared on October 29, 1937.

II   The Chute

Like *The Foundry*, *The Chute* is based on remembered experience; it is fictionalized autobiography. For the major part of the story (of the fifty-seven chapters, forty-two are mainly about the mail-order company and fifteen about the Sussman family), Halper goes back to his job as an order-picker at the Philipsborn Mail-Order Company for his study of the predatory nature of industrial life in one of America's unusual economic enterprises. In it, he dramatizes "the rapacity of big business" and shows, with devastating irony, how it entraps all and consumes some with its intolerable speed and noise, how it exploits man's energies through economic injustice, how it maims the body and distorts the mind. The essential concern of the novel is with moral issues and psychological effects—with hypocrisy and greed, with fear and anxiety, with frustration and loneliness, with personal and public losses that degrade and even destroy men's lives.

Partly a *Bildungsroman*, *The Chute* tells the story of young Paul Sussman, whose experiences are not unlike those of Halper. Sussman has grown up on Chicago's West Side, worked in his father's tobacco store, read a great many books, graduated from high school, and dreamed of becoming an architect. He knows little of the world outside, of love and hate, of competition and greed, of the way people live their lives. Working for twelve dollars a week, he takes the job of order-picker as a temporary measure until, with the help of his parents and with money that his sister Rae saves from her job in Uncle Julius' shirt factory, he can attend architectural school.

Although his job consumes both time and energy, his dream lingers, even dominates his thought and actions. He reads the biography of Louis Sullivan, the architect, and is inspired; he listens to the promptings of Mr. Gebhardt, his high-school drawing teacher, and gathers confidence from his newly found factory friend, Rosanna Puccini, a shoemaker's daughter, who becomes a faithful and affectionate partner in both his dreams and his life at the factory. Though the dream of becoming an architect is aborted by a wrong, perhaps even unnecessary, decision to remain at the factory, he has acquired an insight and a confidence that his factory experience with architectural and geometrical patterns has given—the circular chute, the corners and angles of counters and racks and packages, the maze of aisles, the computation of goods and accounts, the ambiguities of man's thought and behavior. The tortuous curves and darksome squares serve as both obstacle and achievement as man threads his precarious way through the world of the machine that is terrifying for all and rewarding for only a few.

Young Sussman's growth develops against a broad canvas of characters that includes owners and managers and workers of all types, nationalities, and political persuasions; that embraces the ambitious, the prejudiced, the coveteous, the hopeful, and faithful; that reaches out to the families and friends of those whose lives are affected by the Golden Rule Mail-Order Company, Department 2, and by the "gray-cemented West Side streets, along which the wind of destiny doth blow." Although *The Chute* tells something of the history of mail-order houses and of their contribution to the life of rural America, its main concern is with the moral and economic bankruptcy of an organization that pays little attention to individual human needs and values.

As in *Union Square* and *The Foundry*, Halper plots the story partly around the seasons. *The Chute* begins in mid-January and ends shortly after the following New Year. Spring and summer and autumn become decisive forces in the lives of the workers, affecting both their personal lives and bringing seasonal changes to the sales and services with which they must cope. Halper divides the novel into two parts of nearly equal length. Part One brings the end of summer, a reaping of bitter fruit for both the Golden Rule Company and the Sussman family, as the two plots, never really connected except through young Paul, are developed simultaneously. At the Company's annual picnic on the shores of Lake Michigan, one of the "checkers" is drowned; after weeks of persuasion Rae Sussman finally agrees to sleep with her lover Moe Weiner, who drives a laundry wagon. Part Two ends with the coming of the New Year that brings bankruptcy to Golden Rule and job losses for all. Rae's marriage, clouded by broken promises and the violation of personal values to which her parents and most Americans still subscribed, and Paul's love for Rosanna are a brightness that follows in the wake of rain and shifting winds, "beating out their autumnal monotones" and bringing a darkening winter gloom that envelops all.

Relying on techniques that had served in *Union Square* and *The Foundry*—a jazzy and rhythmic sentence; a specific place as unifying factor; a large cast of characters; a detailed description of person, place, and behavior as explanation of the character's inner thoughts and private dreams—Halper sharpens his use of a controlling image by focusing on a particular thing in a particular place. The actual and symbolic center of the novel is the mail-order chute, the "huge cylinder, measuring about twenty-five feet in circumference," which runs from floor to floor and receives the packages from various departments. Both literally and figuratively, it consumes the energies and lives of the people who work with it. A kind of objective correlative, the chute is clearly an integral part of mail operations, the summary of all that goes into preparing orders for shipment. Its power, inscrutable and terrifying, shapes and dominates the lives of all those who work at Golden Rule. Its way of life is essentially destructive, for it reduces man to near animal existence.

Halper's use of animal imagery in describing man's relation to the economic system catches the fear and anxiety of the 1930's:

There it stood, huge and sinister, its mouth open, while Killer Howard worked. Suddenly Big Stella reared her head again, like a stallion, shouting above the bells. "The nine-o'clock orders, the nine-o'clock orders!" . . . As the furious ringing of the bells continued, Killer Howard stuck his head inside the hole, shaking his fist. "Shut up, shut up!" he cried, then went back to the tables for another load. . . . The Killer's eyes, shiny and nasty, made him look like a rat. Paul stood staring at the huge cylinder, wondering what it was. There it stood, its iron mouth wide open, demanding to be fed. There it stood, a monster, insatiable, its gullet yawning for more goods.[5]

Whether worker, young executive, owner—even those who honor it most—all those at Golden Rule fall prey to its indifferent and insatiable power. Nor is the chute a local condition. Cursing the whole set-up from top to bottom, Old Cohen, the philosopher of Department 2, declares, "America is nothing but a big chute!" (388).

Time dominated life in *The Foundry*; speed, a variant of time, and sound dominate, even determine life at Golden Rule. Speed is the cornerstone of business policy. The packages zoom down the chute; the floor becomes a "turmoil and frenzy" of "rigid routine." The scoreboard tallies each order-picker's amount; "Any man who isn't satisfied can go get his time!" (193). Speed, the employer's ideal of good work habits, consequently becomes the aim of any employee who wishes to remain on the job. " 'Well, that's better,' " the buyer

Myerson tells little Kirby, the stock boy, " 'you're counting the stock faster now' " (101). Jack Sidell, assistant buyer, "looking at the order-pickers half-trotting in and out the aisles, . . . wondered which one would make his way up as he had" (104).

Thus Paul Sussman, with little thought other than that of keeping a job, is caught in a tangled web of pride and circumstance that holds him fast to the factory's established pattern. In describing the young man's successful achievements, Halper makes his sentences hiss and swing with movement:

He was now a "veteran," almost as fast as Bugs Goldstein, and he imitated that champ's way of swinging his free arm curtly, though for what reason he did so he didn't know. Anyway, it made you look snappier, like you were going faster than you were. Kirby, squatting on his heels and counting stock in the work-shirt section, lifted up his pale face in admiration as Paul flashed by. "You sure are going fast today," he said, "you sure have a good speed." "I can go faster than that," Paul answered proudly. "Just watch me right now." And he began notching up his speed still higher, snatching shirts out of shelves and piling them rapidly along his left arm. (96)

Speed is symbolic: it means that you are conscious and alert; it stands for efficiency, the number of orders that you can deliver. It makes for a kind of ceremonial gladness; "Feed the chute, feed her, your ten-thirty orders are over four minutes late!" (109).

In the weeks before Christmas, the chute roars the loudest. For ten and twelve dollars a week, fifteen- and sixteen-year-old boys and girls work with superhuman energy getting the orders out. When they work overtime, they are paid only if they work after eight o'clock, although the company gives each worker fifty cents for supper. As the owners see it, speed is the answer to the labor problem; as the workers know, speed is the means of holding a job, the road to their own personal and ecomomic salvation. As Bugs Goldstein says, "The main thing is to run your legs off, to give the company the old krick-krack-krizoo!" (18)

As the chute demands speed to maintain life, so it gives back noise, and the noise of machine-dominated America echoes from the pages of the novel. Noise is everywhere—in the "loud ping" of the time clock, the "mysterious sound" of the conveyor belts, the scream of voices on the job, even at home and at parties, the crash of trucks, loading and unloading, the messengers, Wowser and Bowser, on roller skates, wheeling up and down the aisles. But the most soul-shattering sound of all is the chute bell. Vibrant and blaring, ringing like ubiquitous thunder, it regulates the whole madness to strict schedule; it demands that man function like a machine. As the floor manager explains, "It's like a Ford factory, the trick is not to fall behind. We have to send the orders down the chute on schedule so that the assembling won't get balled up, see? That's why the chute rings, to give us the signal. See?" (17). The bell, like that of Pavlov, conditions through trained response; from the maze of counters and shelves, the managers and buyers and workers, like obedient animals, make material offering and even human sacrifice to an indifferent monster that willingly consumes all. Before its omnipotent capacity, all men are victims. Escape is no easy matter. The most penetrating of all sounds for Henry David Thoreau was solitude; for contemporary man, speed and noise have become so much a way of life that solitude seems merely the refuge of inertia.

Man's constant struggle to outwit his own inventions and imaginings—the machine, desires, prejudices—makes for organizational and personal problems that yield fewer gains than losses. For Helen Flagg and Eve Liebman, life is competition, whether in checking the greater number of packages and orders or in dating every new order-picker who comes on the floor. Eve's death at the annual picnic results partly from accident and partly from exhibitionism. An excellent swimmer, she has gone out too far in an effort to impress Dewey Craighurst, the only college man among the order-pickers; he could not have cared less about the affair. For Mrs. Shumway and, later, for Miss Dawson, their dependence on Emmet Mangan, floor manager and ex-pro football player, as their friend and lover is fraught with lies and deception. Mood and whim dictate whether he meets one or the other or simply gets drunk. Yet he is willing to lie to protect Jack Sidell, the assistant buyer in Department 2. Sidell has hidden back orders instead of filing them, a violation of every code of business ethics. Since Mangan is leaving Golden Rule to take a teaching job, he accepts the blame himself. His deception helps Sidell, but a greater fate awaits all of them. The Company has fallen into bankruptcy.

But there are failures and miscalculations everywhere. Rae Sussman, relying on a device mailed to her in a plain envelope from the Golden Rule Mail-Order Company, discovers that she is pregnant. The buyer of men's furnishings, believing that he can depend on Golden Rule for a better deal, refuses a job with another firm in Omaha, hangs on to a promise, and loses both his job and his life. Fuerstein, the young labor organizer, is finally exposed when the assistant buyer threatens one of the order-pickers to tell what he knows or be dismissed. Paul Sussman gives up becoming an apprentice architect because the pay is less, only to stay on with a company that fails in a few weeks.

With the holiday season, the work load increases, but sales falter. In a hierarchical organization that is medieval in operation, the owners assert their power. Since they determine hours and wages, hire and dismiss employees—sometimes on whim—coerce them into working overtime without pay, they now call the police when the company's interests are threatened by union organizers. As the owners drive the overseers, so the overseers drive the workers. Authority is only allowed to trickle down. When incoming orders slacken or new recruits fail to achieve, workers are immediately dismissed and, when necessary, replaced with fresh recruits.

In *The Foundry* Halper had dramatized the effectiveness of organized labor in the battle for human rights. In *The Chute* organized labor has made small headway amongst the young and needy workers of Golden Rule. The owners warn and cajole; they urge workers to report anyone who is thought to be working "against the general welfare of the many." They appeal to the young people's "comradeship and good feeling," to their "true spirit of American cooperation and perserverance" (404).

Whatever Fuerstein, the professional labor organizer, can accomplish must be done in secrecy and against great odds. Before his exposure by Sidell's cousin, he has made slow and uncertain progress. His trustworthy allies are few—Paul Sussman, who becomes one of the floor's leaders; Big Bill Dorpat, the receiving clerk, who believes in joining a union at once and seeking the protection of the National Labor Relations Board. Perhaps Old Cohen, presser and the floor's philosopher, is more realistic. He is with them, but he tells Fuerstein that the young workers at Golden Rule dare not strike because they and their families are hungry. Besides, most of them are only transient, staying either until they get a better job or, more likely, until they are fired. As Cohen says, "with the weak you can do practically nothing, better organize the strong" (362).

Nonetheless, Fuerstein has gone about his job, trying to educate "the kids," who can't tell "a real genuine union" from a "stool-pigeon company union." Although he knows his Marxism and the Party line, his appeals, like those of the Company, are to "human rights" and "good citizenship." He tells them:

What I meant was that organization isn't enough. Something belongs to you and you ought to know what it is. This is your country and you're its future citizens, and when you put up a fight for better working conditions and human decency you ought to feel that you're making this country a better place to live in. I say, something belongs to you, the right to live honestly and decently and not to be driven up and down these aisles like a pack of dogs. You're Americans and it's your birthright and you ought to be conscious of that fact. When you organize and ask the bosses for better wages and fairer working conditions, you're not asking for favors but for what rightfully is your due. (386)

But unlike the Company spokesman, Fuerstein tries to educate them. He urges them to think, to evaluate, to question the meaning of such words as "loyalty" and "patriotism" and "Americanism." He talks of our "cut-throat age where the technique of the big boys is to drown the real issues under a barrage of windy phrases. . . ." He appeals to their dignity, "None of us here are slackers, we're willing to work, but we don't want to be speeded up like dogs. We want decent hours, decent wages, and a chance to go home without feeling dead tired every night" (387).

Although Halper clearly defines the social and economic problems of both worker and owner, he also sees that the fundamental difficulty lies with the nature of man and is essentially moral. Mr. Gebhardt, Paul's drawing teacher, voices the argument; the problems of the human condition come from man's dishonesty. He tells Paul:

This is the age of hypocrisy, and how long it'll last nobody knows—but perhaps for a long time. The age has just started but has already begun to manifest itself in every walk of life. . . . When the mask begins to slip off, they begin to trot out lies. Every opponent of untruth and injustice begins to find himself a target, he cannot escape. . . . Labor, of course, will be the hardest hit. Labor will see hypocrisy, during the next few years, in so many disguises that it will begin to think the employing class has gone into the theatrical profession. (455)

Sympathetic to the labor movement, certainly to the needs of the laborer, Halper sees that any solution to the problems on either side depends on the honesty, sincerity, and integrity that the "golden rule" demands. Without moral commitment man can expect a continuing battle between those who have power and those who want and deserve a share in decent living.

As the Golden Rule Company tumbles toward financial ruin, the owners, like the workers, search for ways to maintain their solvency. The use of radio advertising says less abokt habits of self-reliance and integrity than about last-ditch efforts to achieve big-volume sales. From the beginning of broadcasting, advertising became standard practice. By the 1930's, many programs were following a familiar format that had turned Broadway and Hollywood stars into modern hucksters. Golden Rule has engaged Rex Bingo, the currently popular crooner, who sings and caresses the latest popular song, accompanied by the Golden Rule orchestra. The "mellow-toned announcer" plugs various Golden Rule products to an unseen audience of millions who are urged to rely on a company that provides, as their motto says, "Honesty—Service—Integrity." In saluting the new retail unit in Birmingham, Alabama, the announcer avoids any ugly little fact that could mar the illusion of doing to others as you would have them do unto you. He says nothing "of the industrial warfare of the community, nor of the murdered organizers or the company towns incorporated within the city limits to escape municipal taxation." He talks only of jasmine and magnolia; a quartet sings "Old Man River" (314). Halper's criticism of this aspect of the American scene is blatant and obvious, but amusing.

The broadcast heralds the advent of failure. The executives of Golden Rule monitor the program in old EG's private office with satisfaction. They lean back in comfortable chairs, sipping brandy, smoking cigars, munching sandwiches that Mrs. Quirt, who has stayed after hours, brings from the cafeteria. Afterwards, EG and the head buyer leave through the silent corridors, going past the hooded machines that look like "darkened gravestones," and speed away in their chauffered limousine. Blanketed against the night's dampness, old EG stares out at the "huge blocks of darkness" and at the "big white building," those solid squares that seem secure against the horrendous and powerful movement of the huge round chute. There "against the murk of mist, [the building] stood huge and monolithic, rearing up fort-like from its foundations, with its north wall blazing out the company's message, 'HONESTY-SERVICE-INTEGRITY,' to the hurrying winds above the city" (317). The hurrying winds are all but winning the battle. As the limousine descends into the darkness, shielding and protecting the "owners" from the very world they have helped to create, the message seems only facade—behind lies the fragmentary dreams, the broken values, the ironic meaning of a motto that mocks at both owner and worker. Neither side wins, but the owners are privileged to ride away in secrecy and comfort.

The end of Golden Rule comes with seasonal and cyclical swiftness. The stock inventory is not sufficient to satisfy the bankers; the Company, consumed by a larger, perhaps more voracious chute, must close its doors forever. In a frenzy of fear and insight, Mr. Myerson, having been tricked and duped with promises of a new job, sees at last "the deep treachery of his superiors, their base betrayal. . . ." (547). As he tries to compose himself, he sees that the green suit, which has been substituted on order after order, has returned for, he believes, the forty-third time. He tears it from the rack, rips it to pieces, and throws them down the chute. As the bells jangle in a final tune-up before the electrician turns them off, Myerson is in a frenzy of fear and anger to silence them. He climbs on a pile of boxes; they give way and pitch him headlong into the chute itself. "Do I hear ringing?" asks one of the buyers somewhere in the building. But the ringing, the noise and sound, has stopped. Now the place literally "is as silent as a tomb," and the lack of sound proclaims the truth about a company whose slogan was only masquerade. The place has served, rather, as an agency of dishonesty, deception, and death.

With the failure of the Golden Rule Company, only a few human relationships remain intact as workers and owners make their final descent into the night. Having completed final negotiations, the owners can still ride away in their limousine. Big Bill Dorpat waits patiently for Mrs. Quirt. Paul Sussman and Rosanna leave together; they walk around the building that is "white and sepulchral," trying to "tease it" back into its former existence. They cross over to the other side of the street, acting as if nothing had happened, walking on as if their world had not crashed. Perhaps it had not. Arriving at Paul's home, "bright-eyed from the frost," they are evidence to his father that with endurance and effort man can still win. Sam Sussman is confident and happy; with his daughter properly married and his son, young and energetic, he finds hope in the next generation. As he says in words that may be Halper's own strategy and solution, "The future belongs to them—they're young, they'll fight" (558). Such faith, personal yet religious and still alive in the 1930's, is the faith of an abiding tradition in America that even a chute has never completely destroyed.

III   Critical Reaction

When Halper began writing *The Chute* in 1935, he was reaching back fifteen years into an experience that came alive as a large and comprehensive picture of American urban life of the mid-1930's.

Reviewers still disagreed over his work, misreading it sometimes or reading it with obvious bias. Yet many agreed with Fanny Butcher that *The Chute* was "better conceived and executed" than any of his previous novels, or with N. L. Rothman that "none among Halper's contemporaries can do a better job of carving a novel out of an industry." The Springfield (Massachusetts) Sunday *Union and Republican* thought the novel had "little plot or organization"; Harry T. Moore said the writing was sloppy. Louis Kronenberger thought that the writing had a pictorial quality and that, if the characters "are sometimes badly drawn, they always seem a genuine part of humanity." Harold Strauss declared that "human beings do not matter to him"; Rothman, again, thought that "Halper's first interest has always been people, how they live, what they say, feel, know." The term "proletarian" had dropped out of the reviewers' critical vocabulary, even in the left-wing press.

New Masses had asked Granville Hicks, a first-rate literary critic and a member of the Communist Party, to review *The Chute*. Hicks's long essay dealt with the novel almost wholly as a literary work and not as propaganda at all. Hicks called it a "feat of humanization," but berated Halper for over-writing, for using many irrelevant details— repetitions, tricks in characterization, intrusive comments, stylistic borrowings from Zola, Dreiser, and Dickens. He praised Halper for his "ability to observe facts truly and to present them so cogently that their significance becomes apparent"; Hicks thought Halper had humanized modern life "by giving us real people in a real environment." Presumably speaking for the *New Masses*, he said nothing about Halper's failure to follow the Party line.[6]

The Chute is a strong and forceful novel, filled with the authentic power of a deeply felt and carefully organized story that tells the effect of noise and speed on man's body, mind, and soul. Halper presents man's existence as a long scream of despair that begins with the blast of the alarm clock in the first sentence to the scream of terror that marks Myerson's death in the final scene at the Golden Rule Company. Just as a city square and a foundry have functioned as representations of American industrial and urban society, so the chute, a more precise and single object, symbolizes the greed and power and indifference of a business world that dominates the lives of bosses and workers alike. The chute's linear and circular shape contrasts visibly with the maze of shelves and squared counters, with the blocks of buildings, the rectangles of streets, the square offices and work rooms. The hustle to respond to the bells and the chute, to the aims and goals of an artificial and inhumane world contrasts with the humanely indifferent turn of the seasons, which remain part of the industrial scene, asserting power through wind and snow and rain and cold as reminders that nature has not been completely subdued. These symbols, concrete and representative, give the story wider meaning. The chute is America; the workers and bosses and owners are everyman; the way of the mail-order house is the human condition.

What makes *The Chute* an outstanding achievement are not only Halper's craftsmanship, but also his use of language. To say that his prose is rough and repetitious—as it sometimes is—is not so much to point to a weakness as to remember that his characters are not intellectual sophisticates or members of the upper class, but ordinary workers, hustlers, small-time foremen and timid vice-presidents, who may be shrewd and clever, even honest and sincere. As their lives are narrow, monotonous, and repetitive, so their talk is often slangy, raw, obscene, a tissue of clichés and shop-talk, of quirks and verbal mannerisms. Although there are exceptions like Paul Sussman, his father, Mr. Gebhardt, who are thoughtful and have individual points of view, most of the characters live by stereotyped phrases that echo their stereotyped lives. Halper's language seems admirably suited to both characters and subject.

In *The Chute* Halper has penetrated behind the facade of the industrial world to show what happens to the inner lives of individuals as they try to cope with injustice and exploitation, with tension and anxiety, with the speed and noise that jangle man's nerves and test his endurance. Although the ending carries a modicum of hope, the world that Halper portrays here is considerably darker than that in his stories and previous novels. In *The Foundry* the union supplied a partial solution to economic injustice; the hero essentially triumphed through his musical abilities. In *The Chute* everyone fails; everyone loses, as if neither man nor nature had yet devised more than temporary solutions for man's poverty and ignorance, his hypocrisy and greed. As Sam Sussman knows, man's love and man's faith may ease the burden; they do not eliminate it.

CHAPTER 6

Remembering Chicago: Part III

O F all the causes that confronted Americans during the 1930's, wrote Samuel Eliot Morison in 1965, the vast majority of them could agree on only one: this country should avoid international commitments and any participation in future wars.[1] Antiwar sentiment and isolationism had steadily increased during the two decades following World War I. Investigations into arms traffic and munitions industries, exaggerated reports on the influence of bankers and business men in wartime operations, a strong popular feeling for neutrality legislation and a repulsion against aggression had created a mood of pacifism that had not existed, historians thought, since the time of Thomas Jefferson.

Artists and intellectuals had joined the growing protest. Writers such as E. E. Cummings, John Dos Passos, William Faulkner, Walter Millis, Irwin Shaw, Edna St. Vincent Millay—to name only a few—described the horrors and terrors of warfare, its consequences, its assault on human dignity and freedom. In Ernest Hemingway's *A Farewell to Arms* (1929), the hero escaped his captors and made a "separate peace." Compared to the names of places, he thought, "abstract words such as glory, honor, courage, or hallow were obscene." [2] For many readers his conclusions had become both their credo and their guide for action. Writers from abroad added to the growing discontent R. C. Sherriff's *Journey's End* dramatized the pity and sacrifice of war on the stage; Erich Maria Remarque's *All Quiet on the Western Front*, no less antiwar for being written from the German point of view, reached millions of viewers through the new medium of talking pictures. Even a frothy Hollywood musical like *Gold Diggers of 1933* included a lavishly staged number about war veterans that featured the song, "Remember My Forgotten Man."

Political parties and groups of varying and sometimes opposite persuasion with ideas and rationales that kept them apart on nearly every other issue were amazingly united in their determination that this country should remain neutral. At the same time, international events were changing political relationships with terrifying swiftness. Japan occupied Manchurian cities in 1931; Mussolini invaded Ethiopia in 1935. In 1936 Hitler marched into the Rhineland; Spain became embroiled in civil war. By the mid-1930's none of these events had yet altered America's determination to avoid entangling herself in European and Asian affairs.[3]

As Halper recalls, "The great trauma of the thirties for many of the country's intellectuals was not the Depression but the tragedy of the Spanish Civil War." [4] Although some volunteers had gone to Spain and some returned to tell of "deadly civil wars raging within the larger civil war," many writers and intellectuals felt simply overwhelmed by the meaninglessness of the destruction and the obvious faltering of democracy. As the mood of pacifism continued, President Roosevelt's approval of expanding the navy in 1938 was decried as unwarranted belligerency on the part of the administration. Hitler's attack on Austria, his annexation of part of Czechoslovakia, the compromises and deceptions of Chamberlain and Hitler in 1938, followed by the Nazi invasion of Poland and the Russo-German Pact in 1939, were events that finally snapped the mood of Americans and brought them to the "brink of war." As the war gathered force in Europe and even before the Japanese attacked Pearl Harbor on December 7, 1941, antiwar groups and their arguments were quietly, then quickly disappearing. Isolationism, no longer fashionable, seemed no longer tenable. What Winston Churchill called "the long, dismal, drawling tides of drift and surrender, of wrong measurements and feeble impulses" had all but vanished.[5] By 1940 Archibald MacLeish had taken the intellectuals and writers to task, calling all those who failed "to oppose" the "destruction of writing and of scholarship" in Europe the "irresponsibles." [6] Once again America found herself entangled in a global conflict.

I   Sons of the Fathers

Halper had begun *Sons of the Fathers* in 1937 at a time when peace had become a hopeless and unwarranted possibility. When the novel was published in October, 1940, the mood of the nation had begun to reverse itself. As if anticipating the reaction of the public to the antiwar attitude of the central character—the narrator's immigrant grocer father—Halper prefaced the book with an "Author's Note" that discussed his aim and some of his ideas. "My sole purpose in writing this book," he said, "was to draw a lifelike picture of an

American family under the strain of war and to present an important
character in American life, the immigrant parent who loves America—and understands Europe." [7] Like the other Chicago novels,
Sons of the Fathers is highly autobiographical; Halper writes about
his family, especially about his father and two older brothers, in a
larger and more sharply focused portrayal of them than he had given
in the stories and other novels that present them under different
names and under happier conditions. Here the theme is man's relation to war and to entangling acts that can and do involve America in
World War I. The two quotations that serve as epigraphs to the novel
carry the burden of argument: the first, a long statement from
Washington's "Farewell Address," asks in part why America should
"entangle our peace and prosperity in the toils of European ambition,
rivalship, interests, humor, or caprice?"; the second, from an unnamed "head of a European state," declares that "War is the normal
condition of Europe." The conflict between man's rational and sensible rejection of war, yet his emotional involvement in it becomes the
major conflict of the novel.

Although the characters' reactions to war involve social and political issues, the novel is less concerned with theoretical argument than
with the making of personal and moral choices. Halper develops the
novel on several levels—the problem of personal relationships between members of the family and between family and friends, where
social and political issues are discussed freely and candidly; the
problem of ethical choices wherein decisions must be made about
public issues in personal and individual ways; the problem of man's
nature, his moral commitment to his inheritance, his inherited or
fateful involvement in evil acts that relate him to outside events. The
deeper meaning of the novel is both cyclical and biblical. With ironic
insight Zellig Bromovitch, the tailor, sees into the moral nature of
man and into the hypocrisy of his actions. He declares:

"Wars should not end with cheering, they should end with weeping! A circus
like this is for imbeciles, not people! But what do they know, these citizens,
these voters! The papers say peace, but there will be no peace, only exhaus-
tion! How can there be peace with ten million men underground, rotting?"
. . . he pointed to the celebrating youngsters. "See them? . . . there won't be
peace for them either! They don't know it but the war has already diseased
them. Remember the words of the prophets! *The sins of the fathers* . . . Yes,
yes they're already tainted! In another generation or so, just wait! The worms
again will be marching! . . . The stink of fine words and patriotism will again
perfume the atmosphere! . . ." (422–23)

The inheritance of "sins" becomes repetitious and timeless; sons inherit their fathers' propensity for war as they fall prey to any disease, and sons in turn perpetuate the endless process. Like all men, fathers and sons must thus pay for their sins in whatever way fate ordains. The deeper meaning of the novel paraphrases and interprets the biblical quotation.

The development of the novel demands its two-part division: Part One, the first third of the novel, belongs to the father, who has emigrated to America from Lithuania at the turn of the century and has come to Chicago to begin life anew. He has already settled down on the city's West Side as a small groceryman, with a growing family and with his dream of living in peace and freedom. Part Two, the major part of the novel, belongs to the sons, to their growth and youthful experiences, to a problem that confronts fathers and sons and people everywhere in America—the growing involvement in a European war and the demands of military service. Although their love and respect for their country do not weaken, neither does their hatred of war, their abiding distrust of military solutions, their love and respect for their father's teachings. The inevitable clash between personal belief and public policy is a conflict between the sensible honesty of the grocer and the emotional opportunism of a majority of fathers, sons, people, who, intoxicated on war, accept both their inheritance and their fate with blind indifference to a suffering world that gathers darkness and weeps.

Like many an immigrant, the Bergmans have come to America with hopes and dreams, not only to escape military conscription, but to live in a nation worth fighting for, a nation so young and strong that "no enemy would dare to come over here to attack us" (9). The birth of their first son signifies that new beginning, and as the family increases to include five sons and a daughter, and as the older sons grow and prosper, their life seems living proof that, although dreams are sometimes not fully realized, the "dreamers" are neither lost for lack of purpose nor alienated for lack of conviction.

With a firm grasp of values and an unswerving belief in the future, the Bergmans buckle down to a life of hard work, trying, as Halper puts it, to hold on amidst such political issues as high tariffs, the silver question, raids on the Federal Treasury, the dominating power of railroads and Wall Street. As Saul Bergman becomes aware of issues that make up part of American life, he holds fast: "Every man should have a job and little businesses shouldn't go bankrupt!" (14). He neither espouses nor knows a particular political or economic philosophy; he lives by personal conviction and the hard-earned wisdom of experience.

The holding fast is not easy; little businesses, as he finds, may easily run into difficulties. After a series of moves and near failures, Saul feels success within his grasp as his Fulton Street Grocery prospers and then fails when a new, more up-to-date store down the block ruins his trade. His nine-month search for a new location depletes his financial reserves and frazzles his nerves; the move to Kedzie Avenue restores his hopes and brings financial stability to the family. But as the "melting pot" of nationalities, the symbolic geography of all America, Kedzie Avenue seems more and more like old Europe with its ambitions, rivalries, and prejudices. As in *Union Square* the street serves as a unity to individuals and their entangling relationships. The community which Saul joins as a Jewish groceryman includes a butcher shop run by a German, a hardware store by a Swede, a fruit stand by an Italian, a drug store by an Englishman, the tailor shop by a Russian. Although the Avenue appears friendly and homogeneous, these city fathers, as Saul quickly sees, have little more in common than the good of their businesses.

As national and international events draw America closer to War, Saul finds himself the outsider that his critical attitude toward foreign wars and his dream of America as the land of peace have made him all along. He keeps his thoughts to himself, discussing his ideas only with Zellig Bromovitch, his tailor friend, whose acerbic comments on the follies of society and the nature of man make him a sympathetic and compassionate listener.

Like some lonely prophet, Saul watches and waits, a tower of sanity and integrity and earned insight. As the street and the world become entangled in a European war, he is relieved at Wilson's reelection to the Presidency. His heart turns cold when men begin appearing on the streets in military uniform. He cannot believe the direction that most "fathers" are taking; he believes their emotionalism will lead to war. Newspapers flame with headlines; the President's war message invokes threatening phrases—"the challenge is to all mankind"; "the rights and liberties of small nations"; "the world must be made safe for democracy!" Saul refuses to join the stampede, but he now concludes that "Wilson is a criminal" (198). "Maybe I'm stupid," he tells his wife,

but to me a war doesn't settle anything; a war only brings miseries to mothers and fathers and ruins whole countries. And in the end it is the common people who pay for it; they pay for the fine statesmen's phrases with tears and taxes, and their blood. (196)

That the "sins" of the fathers will be passed on to the sons is inevitable. Saul's legacy becomes ironic commentary on his own life. His two oldest sons are eligible for military service; his younger children are being taught the glory of the war effort in their classrooms. Nonetheless, he holds to his ideals and to his dream, and he watches and waits.

Much of the story belongs to the sons. Both Milt and Ben (who appear in *On the Shore*) have attended the local schools, helped their father in the grocery store, learned about being Jewish from the taunts of young Irishmen. They are good friends; as boys they have explored the West Side jungle that is their home and playground. They have vastly different personalities. Milt likes "to mix with people and to do things." Ben, more studious, likes "to feel the mystery of the city." At age eighteen, Milt becomes a traveling salesman for a downtown clothing firm. His travels to small unknown towns in Iowa, Illinois, and Missouri sharpen his awarenesses and introduce him to new experiences. He lives in hotel rooms, sleeps on fresh sheets, eats from snowy linen, thinks back on the simple foreign food, the cramped living quarters, the gas lights that he has known at home. He becomes a man of the world. He smokes cigars; on his last trip a woman spends the night in his room.

Never a city hoodlum, Milt turns into a gregarious, likable young salesman, with all the middle-class values of a world he has grown to know. Feelings pull him in two directions. He draws "strangely away from the family," but finds himself "growing more fond of witnessing the ritual of these Jewish holidays with his family. . . . He was bound to Ben and to his mother especially by a strong, emotional tie" (134). In an effort to rid himself of the stigma of the West Side, he joins the young People's Alliance of Temple B'nai Bethel, which takes him to the more prestigious South Side for meetings. At a roller-skating party, he meets Alice Beyer, with whom he falls in love and later plans to marry. Popular with the members, he is elected President of the organization. His achievements are something like the fulfillment of a dream.

With America's entry into the war, Milt looks forward to serving his country with youthful enthusiasm. Already in the draft, he enlists in the Ordnance Corps and, at the same time, enrolls in a course in ordnance training at Northwestern University with the hopes of

qualifying for an officer's commission. Entry into service seems far
from glamorous. To young Americans of the 1930's, Milt's physical
examination may have seemed more caricature than actual reporting.
With World War II, generations of men would remember their initial
experience with mass physical examinations. As Milt recalls, "It
wasn't that they wanted us for the Army that made me feel sick, it was
the way we were standing around while they looked us over like
cattle . . ." (218). He has been firmly caught in an entangling alliance
that his father had always warned against.

Ben's experience with the war takes a different turn. Sensitive, a
dreamer, interested in debate and books, Ben graduates from high
school to become an errand boy at six dollars a week until his brother
helps him get a salesman's job with Milt's old clothing firm. Ben, too,
goes on the road; at Lincoln, Nebraska, he meets a girl whose brother
has just returned from the fighting in France. He has been blinded.
". . . run away," he tells Ben. "Take a boat to the South Seas, or
Chile, or Mexico" (202–03). He speaks with the authority of experience. Ben, a little frightened, listens and runs. He has learned that
farmers are exempt from the draft; overhearing a man tell of his
homestead in Montana, Ben quits his job as salesman, files a claim,
and heads for the proverbial unknown to become a pioneer, like his
father, in a strange land.

In Montana, his world of choice is fraught with obstacles. The
townspeople eye him for a slacker, sell him shoddy materials, take his
money without wincing. He is lonely, thoughtful, miserable. A visit
from Milt partly reassures him, but when the government no longer
exempts farmers, he knows the jig is up. He sells what little he has
back to those who fleeced him and returns home.

In Chicago he finds the draft more easily outwitted than in Montana. He has many helpers. The draft office has lost his registration. A
new winter coat from his old clothing firm, made available to the
officer on the draft board, helps him become a government inspector
of army uniforms in a clothing factory on the South Side. Ben's
services are invaluable. The army has been returning shipments of
uniforms because of shoddy workmanship that competent inspection
would have eliminated long ago. The officers for whom he works are
ill–trained and mostly indifferent to the war effort, but they are
grateful for Ben's expert knowledge. As he takes care of the faults,
they can spend more time at the canteen. Their growing insults and
excessive demands are the price he pays for remaining a civilian.
Ironically, he makes a necessary contribution to a war in which he
does not believe, yet cannot escape.

As the war fever increases, Kedzie Avenue reflects the fears and prejudices of the world's accumulated past. The English barber hints that all Germans should be returned to their fatherland; the Italian fruitman stops buying his paper from the German newsman. The beauty parlor becomes a front for prostitution. People boycott the German's butcher shop. Every merchant is urged to buy Liberty Bonds, to support the Red Cross and the Salvation Army, and to display a "service flag" with a star for every son in service. Newspaper headlines report the latest atrocities, and many people believe them. Federal agents search for wireless sets and possible sabotage. Prices of food and clothing increase rapidly; for his special friends even Saul Bergman puts aside a little sugar or a can of sardines. At school the younger Bergman children learn to shout war slogans. As Bromovitch says, "The whole neighborhood now is full of patriots. There's so much patriotism about I get drunk every time I stick my nose out my shop and smell the air" (322). From a nearby rail station come the sound of troop trains and the shouts of last good-byes. Each day becomes a test of Saul Bergman's sense and sanity.

When young Milt Bergman joined the service, he had confidence both in himself and his country; now his experiences with army life have left him with a feeling of frustration and a sense of loss. The routine of army training, the endless lectures on guns and patriotism, the monotonous life of the barracks, and the unfulfilled promises of ever becoming a commissioned officer remind him of freedoms already lost. He has begun to question ways and means. As he wanders alone toward the outskirts of the reservation, remembering his former life, he gains perspective. As a salesman he had traveled around Chicago in his own car like a free and trusted agent. Here, most of the Company is made up of college men, who have in their own subtle and snobbish way excluded him from their circle. Although he excels as a soldier, he is friendless and lonely. Still weak from a surgical operation, he can neither lift heavy crates nor stack arms without pain.

Being home on furlough only strengthens Milt's growing dissatisfaction. The present seems so unreal, the future so uncertain. With his reassignment to Camp Shelby, Mississippi, the prospect of overseas duty increases. Hans Steubig, his new-found friend, voices their anguish. "Yes, but why must we go over? And why are the others already there? And why is everybody in Europe in the trenches? And why are they fighting?" (338). The attempt to answer these simple questions enables Milt to see that he is merely "repeating words and phrases, which he did not know if he believed, or disbelieved,

himself " (339). Was he beginning to think like Ben and his father?
Was there any sense or value in Moe Kaplan's death at sea? His
mother's illness with a "strange summer cold" causes him to exagger-
ate the truth; he persuades his captain that her illness demands his
presence.

His return to Chicago brings a reversal in his attitudes. He listens
carefully to Ben's arguments that war cannot be justified by high
sounding phrases—"just cause" and "safe for democracy"—but only
by the defense of liberty and freedom. He visits Ben's high school
alumni club and realizes that the principal's lofty speech contains only
empty platitudes. He begins to see the sense of his father's conclusion
that "there is no solution to Europe, that there'll always be wars
there" (370). The feverish pitch of life on Kedzie Avenue frightens
him. The visit to Moe Kaplan's parents, still in mourning for their
son's death, leaves him quiet and thoughtful. The prospect of his
younger brother having military training in grade school convinces
him of the evil power of propaganda. He concludes that Ben and his
father are right. America has entangled herself in a war that will settle
nothing, a war that will only bring misery and pain to all sides.

At the special meeting of the B'nai Bethel Temple honoring young
men in service, Milt presents his new point of view. What he tells the
shocked audience—the many fathers and their sons—is derived, not
from the creeds and arguments of any political or intellectual group,
but from a son's honor and respect for his immigrant father, who had
lived in jeopardy and made sacrifices to come to America. To escape
military conscription and service in aggressive and useless wars, Saul
Bergman had hidden in boxcars, bribed guards into smuggling him
across frontiers, braved personal peril and the prospects of prison.
Milt reminds his audience that America has not been invaded;
citizens' homes are not being sacked and destroyed. He tells the
audience that, like most soldiers, he is lonely and confused. "I realize
that this is war, and these things must be endured, but I, as well as a
lot of other men, don't really know what we're fighting for. . . ." The
listeners are stunned. ". . . as I see it, this country has been dragged
into a war which doesn't concern its people at all . . . and a lot of fine
words have been put forth to cover things up . . ." (383). He recalls
that George Washington told us to keep out of European affairs, but
the audience screams at him. The Rabbi, once his friend, orders him
off the platform.

Milton Bergman's death in France underlines the kind of senseless emotionalism and trick thinking that his father had warned against, the outcome his father had feared. What sins had descended to the next generation? The irony is that although Saul had escaped military service and had come to seek freedom, he had lost his son to the very war machine that he had tried to outwit. Are the sins of man but part of his nature? Must accounts be settled—an eye for an eye? What wisdom could have saved Saul a sacrifice, his son a death? The follies of another father's son attest the irony—the Bergman's cousin, crazy Sammy Stein, returns a hero. He had falsified his age to join the Canadian forces, been wounded in battle and decorated for heroism. A trapeze artist in civilian life, he often visited the Bergmans, stole money from Mrs. Bergman—although he finally repaid her—flashed in and out of their lives with careless ease. Defining his own rules of honesty, he had known little of honor himself, but his achievements are no less honorable, his deeds no less heroic. Old Bromovitch offers Saul some comfort, "Give thanks that you have other children, who have been spared from the butchery. May they comfort you in your old age, so that you will not know the bitterness of loneliness . . ." (429).

Sons of the Fathers is less the story of isolationism—although it is that—than of man's love of peace in a world where hatred and prejudices have given way to war, and where war, like sin, has infected all and has demanded payment in sacrifices and burnt offerings. Saul Bergman was no pacifist; he well knew that the lover of peace might find it necessary "to resist and die rather than to submit and live." But, like George Washington, he thought it unwise for us to implicate ourselves by artificial ties with foreign nations in petty politics and friendless friendships. Whatever wisdom he may have passed on to his sons, neither his son's death nor his own could have denied the sanity of his sense.

The novel begins in light and ends in darkness. When they came to America, the Bergmans had every reason to celebrate the birth of their eldest son with thoughts of joy and words couched in the imagery of light. Their son's birth embodied their new hopes and splendid ideals. The celebration of the armistice that brings cheering and screaming up and down Kedzie Avenue and proclaims the beginning of peace falls on the Bergmans like a leaden echo and brings only a great silence. ". . . and in the street, and in the parlor, the darkness began deepening" (431). By the time *Sons of the Fathers* was in print, World War II was already underway; the darkness on Kedzie Avenue had become a shadow that extended around the world.

II *Reaction and Criticism*

Most readers and reviewers in 1940 looked on *Sons of the Fathers* as propaganda against America's entry into the war. James T. Farrell denounced the novel as political isolationism; he said the writing was slipshod and styleless, the characters superficial and stereotyped, the political comment and social criticism naive, inaccurate, and insufficient. Barbara Giles thought it revealed very little understanding of World War I, which had mainly been concerned with a class struggle, not a struggle of nationalities. Harold Strauss said the novel was "For Isolationists Only," but he praised Halper's warm and intimate handling of characters, his accurate use of historical events. Some reviewers praised his story-telling ability, but roundly criticized his sloppy use of language; one critic said the prose was more "pedestrian than ever." [8]

Sons of the Fathers is not Halper at his best. Although the novel is mainly concerned with the life and ideals of the immigrant father, a major part of the story portrays the growth and development of the sons and the changes that war brings to Kedzie Avenue. The two parts are, of course, related, but the episodic development of the two centers of interest makes for an organization of the novel that is more loosely controlled than in *The Chute* and *The Foundry*. Whereas in his other novels the action is largely confined to a "collective" place, here the action ranges far beyond the "avenue" and family circle. The sentences, many of them wordy and tedious, lack the snap and explosiveness of the earlier writing; the scenes, rife with social history and filled with carefully observed detail, lack the dramatic qualities of the earlier stories about the same characters of that same West Side world. But here, drawing upon familiar territory, Halper has envisioned a world that has both darkened and deepened.

In focusing on the story of an immigrant "father" who believed in peace and on his sons who inherited his beliefs and tried to live by them, Halper weaves personal memories into history. Some of the episodes are warmly personal, such as the father's confrontation with the school principal about the children fighting; the celebration of the Passover holiday; the memorial prayer for Milton in the Bergman's parlor. But other episodes contain a large amount of social and urban history—the reaction of people on Kedzie Avenue to the assassination of Archduke Franz Ferdinand; the hysteria of a war rally as it turns into a mob; the opportunism of Kedzie merchants as they prosper through wartime inflation; the outbreak of sickness and epidemics.

As historian and artist, Halper had set out, as he says, "to see life clearly, and as whole as may be, and then to tell the truth about it." He wanted, he said in the "Author's Note," "to write a novel—and not a tract." In a sense he has done both. Although the novel contains social and political criticism—the father's belief has political implications—the basis of Saul Bergman's thinking is moral and religious. The novel shows what happens when the sensible idealism of a practical man comes into conflict with such powerful and determinate forces as public opinion, greed and hypocrisy, prejudice and fear, revenge and expediency. Although one son changes his attitudes toward the war and moves closer to his father's beliefs, Saul Bergman holds fast to an ideal that attests his sincerity and strength of character.

Sons of the Fathers portrays life in World War I, but Halper's concern is with the logic of thought and response in all wars—what happens to political justice and moral commitment? What happens to the concept of honesty and integrity? What happens to man's dedication to the ideals of peace and freedom? As Halper knows, answers to these questions are endlessly complex; solutions, perhaps impossible to achieve, lie with neither isolationism nor involvement, but with man's moral commitment to a position that enables him to live with his past and with his own nature and, at the same time, to endure his dreams and his belief in freedom and independence.

III   The Little People

Halper published *The Little People*, his last novel about Chicago, in October, 1942. America was already deeply involved in wars all over the world. The nation's industry had begun producing quantities of war material, which, with millions of men in the armed services, helped in solving the problems of prosperity and unemployment. Although *The Little People* is a novel about business and urban life, a novel of social criticism and ethical problems, it has nothing to do with war, with proletarian propaganda, with strikes or labor unions. Even when published, the novel made the 1930's seem part of the distant past. In a sense, they were.

For the setting of the novel and some of the characters, Halper remembered back nearly twenty-five years to his experience as errand boy at John T. Shayne & Company, an exclusive fur and clothing store, located at that time on the State Street side of the old (the third) Palmer House, before the hotel was torn down and rebuilt in the mid-1920's.[9] In shifting the time of the story to the 1930's, he had not so much invented details for the plot as he had drawn on fragments of experience that he had had in many jobs. He set to work on the novel in late autumn, 1940, carefully making notes and organizing the material, paying more attention to the rhythms of sentences than to niceties of syntax. The novel breaks no new ground. As in *The Chute* and *The Foundry*, here he makes an institution the container or unifier of setting and action. The fairly large canvas of characters (around thirty) contains many of the same types of workers and employers that Halper had used before, and he treats them, not as economic forces, but as individuals, some weak or timid, forceful or self-willed, yet all of them caught by quirks of circumstance and trapped by faulty judgments.

The Little People is the story of the employers and employees and even a few customers of Richard T. Sutton & Company, well-known for its Hats, Furs and Gentlemen's Haberdashery. For years the store has occupied several floors on the State Street side of the Potter Hotel, a distinguished but decaying landmark, now slated for demolition. In plotting much of the action around the destruction of the building and the subsequent removal of the fur company to a new location on Upper Michigan Avenue, Halper shows how time and progress have catapulted man into a new and wondrous mechanical world that actually affects all, but spells disaster for only a few.

Using a technique to be found in his other novels and stories, Halper relates "closing" of the old store and the reestablishment of the new to the eternal cycle of seasonal change. Ubiquitous and inexorable, the seasons turn through the story like a wheel of time, indifferent to consequences, reliable as change. The story begins in winter and ends, nearly a year later, on Thanksgiving Day. Spring brings a rush of sales, a burst of spring fever; summer, the doldrums and after-hour escapades. Autumn, abundant with new merchandise and new problems, brings September winds and "the blues again, those dreary, rooming-house blues." [10] As cold weather and the wrecking crews move in, November brings rain and destruction, the end of the old "order" and the beginning of the new. Place and time determine part of the organization: Parts Two ("Today is Sunday") and Five ("Thanksgiving Day") are the detailed recounting of what happens to individuals on a single day; hence the action takes place in many parts of Chicago, in the streets, the parks, the amusement centers, in boarding houses and apartments; here the narrator reveals the private lives and inner thoughts of the characters. Parts One ("Beneath the Stairs"), Three ("Spring Is Here,") and Four ("Death and the Latest in Millinery") introduce the people at Sutton's and portray their collective and public lives.

On a "normal" working day, the characters are beset, not so much with problems of economics and labor as with problems of self and human relations. The hatter's wife is sick and dying. Mr. Dawes, one of two bosses, has a weepy eye when he gets excited. George, the night watchman is crippled. John Narhigian, the Armenian shipping clerk, eats only a vegetarian diet. Odessa, the black helper in furs, is suddenly dismissed when Mr. Larch, who simply hates her color, accuses her of turning away customers. Mr. Cecil Leroy, homosexual, is jokingly tolerated by his fellow workers. Helen Browning in millinery, seeking an affair with Mr. Chetwood, finds herself pregnant and Chetwood gone. Al Grimes, elevator operator, seduced by a prostitute at their rooming house, catches venereal disease. The new salesman, Major Twirlinger, flutters the pulses of women admirers, telephones Miss Revere of Millinery, but settles for a night with Miss Boyle, saleswoman. At Sutton's the little people, like all people, are beset with sicknesses and dreams and desires; with personality clashes, infatuations, and deceptions; sometimes even with the sympathetic and confiding gestures of love and friendship. Many of them seem rootless, as if they had no past, a doubtful future, at best only a present. Isolated, lonely, they drift; rarely do they find a true friend or the compassionate understanding of another. Rather, as Halper sees, the lives of men weave themselves into intricate and subtle patterns which contain neither abiding answers nor solutions, but only consequences that must be accepted and endured.

Of the several floors of "Not the Largest Store But the Most Exclusive," much of the action is concentrated in the basement of Sutton's where, "beneath the stairs," the inner workings of the store may be seen. Here hats are cleaned and "conformed"; furs, umbrellas, canes, expensive haberdashery are sent for packing and delivery. Here the chauffeurs and delivery boys wait, here salespeople from departments upstairs congregate to check on orders, sneak a smoke, drink coffee, make friends, and arrange meetings. They report the gossip and news of little events that make up the inner lives of people. Nick, the new boy in haberdashery, tells how Mr. Leroy made advances toward him, even tried to "touch" him. Mr. Twirlinger, the seedy new salesman in the fur department, quickly gains a reputation as a small time romeo. Chauffeurs Hank and Butch, high school graduates from the South Side, chide the delivery boys from the West Side as coming from the "land of the WPA." Word travels fast that a new girl has just been hired in millinery. The gossip, dull and meaningless, sounds like the talk of people everywhere.

When "Mr. Scammel, the one nobody downstairs in the basement liked—rattled the old wooden shafts of the dumbwaiter with the malacca cane" (3) in the first sentence of the novel and calls for Oscar Bresslin, chief hatter at Sutton's, the reader is plunged directly into the inner life of the store and introduced to the one person who merits everyone's respect. The best hatter in Chicago, Bresslin works with speed, skill, and unflagging devotion. With a wife sick and dying, he often comes late to work, but never leaves until the hats are finished. Thoroughly independent, he brings a personal, human touch to his job. Around four every afternoon he makes coffee for himself and his friends. When the management tacks up a sign advising "NO POLIT-ICAL ARGUMENTS ON THE PREMISES," he tacks up his own sign, "Peace on Earth, Good Will toward Men." He berates Al Grimes for talking about the Jewish bookkeeper as "one of 'em"; "What's the matter with Miss Nussbaum? Isn't she a human being like you and me?" (55). His attitudes, humane and just, constitute the moral center of the novel.

Bresslin's personal life is plagued by problems and reverses. He has saved enough money so that he can open his own hat store. Then, his wife dies; funeral expenses wipe out his savings. He has fallen in love with Helen Browning, the girl from millinery, with whom he has coffee at the store. Although she often comes to his apartment and cooks Sunday dinner, she is so infatuated with Roy Chetwood that she may slip out to the corner drugstore just to telephone him. Bresslin remains optimistic, with a kind of blind faith in the future, himself an example of virtue and dignity.

The story of Al Grimes, rootless and restless, is one of waste and losses. Perhaps the major character in the novel, but no hero, he operates the elevator at Sutton's. Hermes-like, he speeds up and down with news and gossip from all parts of the store, reporting his findings to his friends "beneath the stairs." Loud and loquacious, he is one of Halper's best characters, a familiar type of person found in all of his novels. His talk is rapid and up-to-date. " 'Attention, Mister and Missus North America, ships on the high seas, and fellow bean-eaters—' he began," imitating Walter Winchell of radio news fame, "then stopped short as he saw the intent faces around him" (139). Or "This is your faithful State Street correspondent signing off until the next news flash! Please stand by!" (53). Short of stature, energetic, still unmarried at twenty-four, he is snappily dressed in cheap clothes; he hums the latest popular song and keeps his eye on the look-out for tall, good-looking women. Up and down, in and out, he delivers his customers, making chatty comments to them and about them, riding along on his brassy jokes, his endless patter only masking an empty life. He is still the funky kid from Kedzie Avenue who ought to know better.

For Al, Sutton's serves more as a hunting ground than a learning opportunity. He is spurred to rude assertions by Major Twirlinger's success with the ladies. Attracted to Wanda, the new black helper, he tries to assist her in hanging the furs back on the rack, but his actions suggest otherwise. She scorns him, " 'You get away from me. I got a man. I don't need any white trash like you. I got a *real* man, a man I respect . . .' " (125). Scared, he hurries toward the elevator. Or, he discovers the Latin motto that Sutton's uses in its hats—*Otium cum Dignitate*. His search for its meaning reveals ignorance everywhere. Mr. Leroy, a college man, has forgotten "my foreign languages." Al is scornful; "You mean that what you learn in college . . . only sticks while you're there and as soon as you get out you don't know nothin'?" (160) When, after the fifth try at the Chicago *Tribune*, he has the answer—"Leisure with Dignity"—he resorts to obscenities, "That's education for you, they slap three words in a hat which nobody can figure out! . . ." (162). His comment may be true enough, but such discoveries have brought him neither insight nor wisdom.

Having learned little on the job, he fails even more miserably on his own. After hours he seeks friendship at the Hot Swingland Ballroom. An expert dancer, he dips, contorts his torso, side-saddles, puts on the heat as the band gives out with the "boogie-woogie, stomp, and Lindy stuff bango style." (43) He searches for "the tall" girl of his dreams. One night he finds her. She drinks the liquor he can't afford, dances a perfect tango and foxtrot, smiles mysteriously. When he takes her home and makes advances, she calls him names and shuts the door in his face. He returns to his cold room at one-thirty in the morning depressed and miserable, defeated and angry. " 'I never find no happiness like other people,' he told himself over and over, taking off his clothes, his lower lip trembling. 'I never get a break' " (48). And he never does.

As a playboy he is inadequate and frustrated. With free tickets to the White City Amusement Park on the South Side, he wanders alone in a maze of side-shows and friendly pickups, hoping for a break. He eats hot dogs and dopes himself with rides. "Every time the cars climbed high over the glittering carnival grounds he screamed out his defiance, his screams lost amid the other screams, his face like a maniac's" (185). His "God, gimme a break" is a prayer or a curse, but at the Dance Hall a break comes.

Although he still seeks the "tall" type, he settles for Betty, a dance partner so sweet and considerate that he falls in love with her. She is hardly as tall as he, but they dance their way into each other's minds and emotions. He takes her home, remembers a yellow door, loses the match booklet on which he wrote her telephone number. He knows neither her last name nor her address. In his frantic search to find her, he spends all his money on advertisements in the personal column of the *Tribune*. He walks the streets of the South Side, looking for a yellow door. In utter frustration and loneliness, he spends a night with Joyce, the prostitute who lives in his rooming house. He catches venereal disease and adds agony to misery. As he stares from his window into the enveloping darkness and senses the chill of winter in the autumn air, he feels the "misery of his own soul's crucifixion" (291). Empty, hollow, sick, without real values or intellectual resources, he has been impelled by immediate desire into a greater anxiety and loneliness than he has ever known.

Plagued by personal problems, Al continues to run his elevator, but the old zing has gone. The gossip about the store barely relieves his misery. Miss Crump has won three hundred dollars in a radio program. Mr. Bottle, hat salesman, has been struck and killed by a bakery truck; no one can remember his first name. Major Twirlinger returns from Detroit, having proved himself the failure that he has always been. Mr. Fandine, the cashier, disappears with three thousand dollars of the firm's money. Lately, Al has been taking a cure for his VD, but he discovers that the doctor is a fake; the green pills, utterly worthless. Then, one night as he ambles along a street on the South Side, he finds the yellow door that he has been seeking. But the light in Betty's room belongs to somebody else. The girl he seeks has already married and left. He has missed her by two days. Some win; Al Grimes always loses.

Preparations for demolition of the Potter Hotel and removal of all businesses including Sutton's runs like a series of shock waves through the last part of the novel. The hotel has had an illustrious history, playing host, as the narrator says, to "second-rate royalty from Europe, presidents whose prestige had been deflated, brilliant gamblers, famous actresses . . . , eccentric rich spinsters, and traction barons whose sins had been whitewashed by handsome gifts to the city's universities" (323). Its demise symbolizes more the end of a way of living than the end of a particular era. Although World War I, the gay spree of the 1920's, and the economic collapse in the 1930's had ended much of the showy elegance, the vulgarity, the conspicuous consumption of American life in the first decades of the century, none of these catastropes had abolished prejudice and ignorance and dishonesty. Nor had they eliminated the phonies who tried to deceive, the over-privileged who sought an advantage, the under-privileged who simply could not manage—the little people at all the Suttons' in the world.

At the new Sutton's, mechanism is the key to progress. The place looks "like a castle." The employees, invited to a preview that has been carefully arranged to take place on their day off, are overwhelmed with the "brillance." The indirect lighting in the modern Swedish showcases makes the windows sparkle like diamonds; the air is automatically cooled; the cash registers and the new elevators are automatic. Photoelectric cells operate the fur vaults, which are protected by a time mechanism and by direct wires "to a central board which in turn informs the police in case of any tampering" (356). " 'My, my, my,' gasped Mrs. Hatch. . . . 'Ain't modern improvements wonderful?' " (353) Even the doorman looks like an "admiral of a Swiss navy" (347). Roosty, unconsciously accurate in his observation, thinks the new store looks "like the Palace Theater!" By the 1930's American business had already acquired the theatrics and methods of huckersterism that later became known as Madison Avenue techniques. As John Narhigian says, "America! . . . What a great, genius country!" (352).

Although the new facilities "beneath new stairs" have been improved, the place is, as Al Grimes says, "no palace down here" (355). With the old furniture and the same sign forbidding political arguments—but newly made in larger letters—and only small street-side windows for ventilation, the place much resembles the old quarters. Upstairs, decoration and safety and comfort have received maximum consideration; below stairs, old errors—not old traditions—have been perpetuated. In reckoning the meaning of change, always complex and ambiguous, Halper has credited the new efficiency and technological advancements that have helped modern merchandising and has duly reported the newspaper's optimism about a healthy economy in the same terms that they had used for the last several years. But there are changes other than those of economic statistics, changes that are simply part of the natural process; if man is to possess complete knowledge of himself and his world, he must be aware of the very nature of change. The weather forecast is bleak, a little foreboding, ". . . chilly, with overcast skies. Wind northeast, changing to east. Colder in evening; at nightfall probably snow . . ." (336). As the wreckers finish demolishing the old establishment and the photoelectric cells guard the new, George, the nightwatchman, is no longer needed.

The Little People begins and ends with Oscar Bresslin, whose moral commitment to people remains unchanged throughout. At the Applegate's christening party, he rescues Helen Browning, sensing that the girl is ill. As he says, "We don't know what life is, or where we are going, but we plug along! And someday, if everybody sweats hard enough, and people learn enough sense to pull together, life will be a little better for all of us!" (394). Oscar does his part. Since Chetwood has run out on Helen Browning, who is carrying his child, Oscar offers to marry the girl and raise the child as their own. He knows that any additional expense shatters his dream of owning a hat shop, but he has no illusions. Suddenly a bright moon gives the new-fallen snow "an enigmatic brillance," but he is philosophic. He knows that clean snow does not last. Although he has failed to achieve his material goal, he comes as close to happiness as men ever do. Halper ends with a metaphor, not a solution—just as a fiery brillance remains in precious stones, even in those "unattainable" ones behind the "jeweler's plate-glass window," so Oscar's dream remains clearly in view and clearly unpossessed.

IV *Reactions and Criticism*

With *The Little People* Halper's position as a novelist was firmly secure. No other writer, said N. L. Rothman, could match his "half-inarticulate talk of the little people, choked with clichés and repressed passions." [11] Isaac Rosenfeld called it "Halper's best book in that it carries itself without prodding, a little vaguer and wiser than heretofore." [12] An unsigned review in *The Nation* declared that *The Little People* "comes out of the same old competent—very competent—realism machine." [13] Lillian Gilkes, reporting for *New Masses*, said that Halper was a "novelist with something to say who says it better than most." [14] She noted his failure to mention labor unions, but her tone was mild. The magazine that had excoriated him eight years before now paid him tribute. The victory was ironic—the Party, not Halper, had changed.

As in the preceding novels and stories about Chicago, *The Little People*, the last of the Chicago novels, shows the changing patterns, the dreary loneliness of urban and industrial life. Halper's use of a historical framework—the demolition of the hotel and the store's removal to new quarters—gives his little people a niche in history, for he penetrates the facade of city life into the moods and reactions, the inner strengths and weaknesses of people, not only in Chicago, but in all of urban and business America. Less violent and less noisy than *The Chute* and *The Foundry*, the destructive element is even more corrosive: sickness and death, ignorance and inadequacy, defeats and losses, the insistence of disease and despair typify the human condition. Nor does Halper try to solve unsolvable problems, except for individuals, who, having made decisions or having had them made for them, may take a direction and manage to endure to the next turning.

As historian and realist, Halper finds heroism in many places, but seldom a single hero. Both Oscar Bresslin and Al Grimes come close to a hero's role, but Oscar has achieved nothing that he did not possess already; Al Grimes possesses nothing that he has ever achieved. Independent of spirit and action, they are colorful and memorable, providing a certain bleak humor to a plot that, like *Union Square*, has the thinness of a musical revue. With a warm feeling for man's foibles and failings, Halper presents another picture of the human comedy that, whatever the variations, is much the same as life in the four preceding novels.

CHAPTER 7

Historian of the Present

"THE Depression," Halper said in *Good-bye, Union Square*, "ended with America's entry into World War II." It brought, he said, "the end of an Era." [1] By the early 1940's, unemployment had all but disappeared; even protesters had stopped advancing on Union Square. With the Russo-German Pact, left-wing thinking had taken new directions. With the attack on Pearl Harbor, the thought of winning the war had consolidated allegiances and brought a unity of effort into the national life. Armed forces personnel were everywhere. The increase in prosperity and the need to wage an all-out war had turned the nation's attention away from social and economic problems. Although many of the social gains of the 1930's had already become part of the life and style of the nation and would remain permanent fixtures after the war, the shenanigans of politicos and of partisan activities, playing upon such human traits as greed and prejudice and ambition, had also left scars on the national conscience.

Throughout these changes Halper had remained a close observer of the shifting scene. Although he had never joined radical groups and seldom debated ideological issues in the public arena, he had been aware of the drift of events, argued social and political issues with friends and editors, attended protest rallies in Union Square and listened to Communist debates in Webster Hall. Whatever the concern with his own past, he had never retreated from the present scene. He had written about contemporary events in *Union Square* and woven their design into the fabric of his Chicago novels.

In "Prelude," a short story which appeared in *Harper's* in August, 1938, he had turned an actual event into a prediction of what could happen to America. His comments on the writing of this particular story reveal his sensitivity to political action and show how his methods of composition mingle moral commitment with social thought and action. What begins as political and social clash becomes moral drama.

110

He had based the story on personal experience, for one day he had witnessed a clash between right and left-wing political factions in New York that involved an attack by Fascist hoodlums on a Jewish news dealer on 86th Street. The event had stunned him. Mingling fact and invention, he recast the episode into a story that is as vivid and personal as anything he has written. He returns to Chicago for the setting, a corner newsstand under the Elevated tracks, and he makes the narrator a thirteen-year-old boy who comes to relieve his father, Mr. Silverstein, who is old and tired. Neither the narrator nor his sister knows that hoodlums from "Gavin's pool-room" have been molesting the old man, throwing rocks and rotten apples. This time the hoods go further; they decide to have "a little fun with the Yids." They pick on the narrator, order him to do some physical exercises. Mrs. Oliver, a customer, urges people to help the boy, but no one comes to the rescue. When the cops arrive, the newsstand has been wrecked. Even so, only Mrs. Oliver is willing to testify against those who committed the acts.

Most Americans in the 1930's had read and known of similar attacks on the Jewish people in Europe, especially in Germany; they were less aware of such happenings in the United States. Halper had compressed the feelings of a generation into a story that comes close to political statement, for it shows the violence and prejudice that had surely served as "prelude" to a world that was soon to erupt into World War II. In language that is lean and spare, he had caught the fear and terror and despair that enervate and destroy a civilization when violence becomes the tolerated instrument of power and authority. He had already written about the racial violence which he had witnessed in Chicago when growing up; here was another episode in the history of man's inhumanity to man. "Prelude" was both a warning and a prediction.

With the beginning of World War II—and the end of the Depression—the major part of Halper's career lay behind him. In less than fifteen years after his arrival in New York, he had become one of the important writers of the decade. Five published novels and nearly fifty short stories attest both a quantity of production and a quality of work that assured him a place in the literary history of the era. As historian and novelist, he had spoken directly to the issues and problems of the period in language that was simple and vivid and free of intellectual cant. But after World War II, his work seemed to belong to the past. His writing had been so closely identified with the

1930's, with the problems and themes of the Depression, with workers and their daily concerns that it had already faded into a fateful past that nobody wanted to remember.

During the next thirty years, Halper continued to produce. The three novels, twenty-five or more short stories and essays, two anthologies, a volume of memoirs, and two unpublished plays have neither redeemed his loss of prestige nor revived an interest in his earlier work. In the stories, the memoirs, the introductory notes to the two anthologies about Chicago, he has returned to his own past, and these form a continuous link with the writings of the 1930's. But in the novels, he writes, not about Chicago, but about the people he has known in New York, about a contemporary and bohemian world that is somewhat removed from the mainstream of American life.

I Urban and Bohemian Life

Halper's last three novels have appeared at widely spaced intervals: *Only an Inch from Glory*, 1943; *Atlantic Avenue*, 1956; *The Fourth Horseman of Miami Beach*, 1966. Although they deal with characters and themes that are reminiscent of those in the Chicago novels, the differences in them are readily apparent. With a smaller number of characters, the last novels are shorter in length, not concerned with workers or factories or the labor situation at all. The earlier novels had been written around a collective symbol; the later novels follow a more traditional form. Although geography continues to play a part in the stories and Atlantic Avenue serves as a title, streets and places function more simply as scene than as symbol.

As in all his writings, Halper focuses on individuals, and in the last novels, his individuals are as lonely and unheroic as his little people of the 1930's. Some of them have jobs, of course, but they mainly live on the fringes of society and certainly can not speak for "all America." As businessmen, writers, gamblers, painters, dancers, con men, simply hangers-on, they keep one foot in a bohemian society or have connections with the criminal world. Love and violence absorb their emotional desires and psychological quirks. Very few of them are consumed with righteous indignation at anything, and no one wants to reform the status quo, let alone overturn it.

Their concerns are love and money; they are devoted to making the fast buck and, whenever opportune and profitable, to pursuing their own pleasures. Sometimes talented and industrious, they connive, gamble, evade the law, dissipate their lives in booze and sexual escapades, which complicate their lives and frequently betray them. They have grown up with the conventional moral code, but they do not hesitate to break it. In pursuing their personal interests, they sometimes find love and happiness, but more often losses and regrets. Frustrated and lonely, tormented by their own feelings of guilt and inadequacy, they are victims of their own emotions and desires. In the Chicago novels, the world is filled with social injustice; in the later novels, the world seems neither just nor unjust, but the people in it are creatures of despair.

Only an Inch from Glory, written during World War II, is not a war novel, but the threat of war and its effect on the characters help in molding their lives. Although there are flashbacks, the story really begins in November, 1941, in "the third year of the war in Greenwich Village—the second section of the World War," [2] and ends a few weeks after the attack on Pearl Harbor—shortly before January 3, 1942. The novel is a short and swiftly moving tale of four young Village bohemians, whose emotional problems and shabby relationships betray their rebellious and romantic attitudes, their loves and hates, their itch for glamour and glory.

Halper's technique in telling the story varies from that of preceding novels. He makes the narrator one of the participants in the action; Frank Keenan tells the story in both first and third persons, basing episodes partly on the diary that Dorothy Lynch left behind after her death and partly on his own observations and memories. As he studies the diary-ledgers, he reviews and reveals the past, "those golden pre-Munich days, during that misty, twilit period when everybody except our statesmen knew the world was teetering on the brink of a precipice over which history was about to plunge" (12). Keenan and Dorothy have left provincial lives in Boston and Sayville, Indiana, but the Village and the golden days are only indirectly accountable for their shabby personal lives and emotional mix-up at a time when everything in the world goes crash.

Keenan has come to the Village to paint and write; instead, he takes a job as credit manager for a hosiery concern. He first met Dorothy Lynch in a drawing class; she praised his work, filled him with the "erroneous nostalgia of accomplishment," and made him feel like a "wonderfully new person." A "spiritual drifter," he falls in love and wants to marry her. Dorothy Lynch has little capacity for making such a decision. After three years of flitting from job to job, from one infatuation to another—from artist to scene designer, from radio writer to alcohol—she establishes a pattern to her life that leads

nowhere. Romantic and infantile, talented and uncertain, still a
chaser of rainbows and illusions, she works in a jewelry store, where
she occasionally creates an original design for a pin or brooch. Her
apartment breathes the "spirit of loneliness and a barren life" (31).
Although Dorothy and Frank have lived with their frustrations and
defeats, Keenan's job has been a way out that Dorothy Lynch's has
not. Even their friends the Gluckmans, married and successful,
cannot help.

Like Dorothy and Keenan, Anne and Sam Gluckman are themselves close to defeat. A press agent for Broadway shows, Sam Gluckman talks like a "composite of Ben Hecht and Noel Coward" (34). He
is talented and clever, but his dream of writing successful Broadway
plays falls short. His manuscript is returned again and again. As
agent-critic, he is harsh and vindictive, outspoken and belligerent,
betraying the petulance of frustrated purpose. Deceitful and unreliable in private life, he cheats on his wife, even calls Dorothy Lynch,
who refuses his overtures and despises him. He hardly deserves
Anne's sensible maternal guidance; she helps and protects him, types
his manuscripts and believes in his talent, but openly longs for
children. When these four come together, drastic things happen.

Their gatherings are public exhibitions of private irritations and
desires. At the opening of a highly rated Broadway play, Sam is
petulant, caustic, loudly vocal against a comedy that the audience
obviously enjoys. During intermission, he voices and pantomimes his
disapproval for all to see. Afterwards, they celebrate at the Cafe Bed
near Sheridan Square, where their friend Max Stein has engaged a
new band with a new drummer so sensational that when the fellow
beats the drum "with such well-timed ferocity his arms looked a blur"
(63). The drumming hypnotizes Dorothy Lynch into writing the
young man an adulatory note that includes an invitation to meet with
him. It marks the beginning of a new infatuation.

For a little while Dorothy and Keenan have drawn together, but
her defection shatters the whole group. Keenan bows out; the Gluckmans rewrite Sam's play, and while the rewriting is doomed to
failure, the working together gives Anne Gluckman a ray of hope for
their marriage. Sam Gluckman is lost on a creative binge of dramatiz-
ing his assertive ego.

Dorothy's affair with drummer Sonny Allen gives her a feeling of
renewal as if being close to success enables her to share in it as her
own. Heedless of consequences, she gives recklessly of herself.
Sonny Allen, egotist and colossal bore, takes what he can get. Mar-

ried at the age of twenty, he willingly leaves his wife and children to
live with Dorothy in happy convenience. Since Sonny comes from
Indiana and says "Aw, shucks," they feel a common background of
understanding. For the umpteenth time Dorothy declares that she
has never "felt this way about a man before," (93) but the infatuation
wanes. As Keenan observes, "She liked to enjoy a person, or a song,
or a drink up to the moment the crest was reached. Then she wanted
to check out. It takes a strong and honest personality to be like that
. . ." (145).

Sam Gluckman's Sunday afternoon party (December 7, 1941)
reunites the four and presents a collection of Hollywood and Broadway types. Each guest has come eagerly expecting to meet a "well-
known personality." The sudden announcement on the radio that the
Japanese have attacked Pearl Harbor quiets the buzz of chit-chat and
backbite. As the party ends, a new and different world has come into
being.

Changes in personal lives and the national scene go hand in hand.
Sam Gluckman, who has learned to pilot a plane and longs to escape
into military service, is rejected by the air force because of age and
bad eyesight. Dorothy Lynch, tired of Sonny Allen, calls an old
novelist friend, a former infatuation, who has forgotten her. But when
she turns to Frank Keenan with the idea of marriage in mind, a "sense
of order" comes into her life. It is too late. At the third meeting of the
"group," a jazz concert at Philharmonic Hall, Sonny Allen's wife
attacks Dorothy and stabs her. "I wasn't meant to be happy," she tells
Anne Gluckman before she dies, and she hasn't been. The orchestra
plays "Good-bye Pretty Baby"; the song is ironic commentary on a
wasted life.

No one wins. All are victims. The ledger-diary tells the story of
their double attitudes and split lives, of plain "Ida" Lynch, who has
journeyed from a little midwestern village to become entrapped by
her own illusions of bohemian life. As Keenan says, "I realized she
had been Ida all the time, no matter how hard she had tried to live
under the romantic cloak of Dorothy" (261). Lonely and frustrated,
her hopes crushed, she has been, in part, as her father says, "the
victim of a big city" (272). The explanation is perfunctory, sociological; Halper dwells on the personal, the psychological.

Lured by the "cupful of glory" that she might even have deserved,
Dorothy has never been able to convert illusions into realities. She
had come to New York believing in her right to follow her own plan,
as if a discipline of some kind would see her through. Her failure to

create, "to find herself," impelled her toward those who had been successful. Seeking an illusion that forever eluded her, she remained always an inch from the glory and fulfillment of her dreams. As plain Ida Lynch she no longer wanted what she had; as Dorothy Lynch she was never able to have what she wanted. Hers is no isolated case; the Gluckmans—even Frank Keenan—have become victims of their dreams and illusions in a world that holds for them only a little assurance.

Whatever hope there is lies with the narrator, with Frank Keenan. His losses have not nullified his capacities to understand and endure his fate in a changing world. He sees that the worship of success, which has destroyed Dorothy and frustrated the Gluckmans, is not unlike the fascists' worship of success and power, a worship that has sanctioned the destruction that is smashing the world to pieces. He also sees that self insight is not achieved amidst the glitter of night spots and parties, but from an intense scrutiny of one's image when alone, "when you go to the bathroom sink for a glass of water and stare at the mirror. . . ." As he says,

The face in the bathroom mirror is yourself, and no matter what kind of face it is, it stares back at you with the unadorned and honest story of your solitary life. . . . it has always seemed to me that those people who live alone in our great cities are like seamen who stand on a lonely deck watching for the evening star. (97–98)

Man's isolation and loneliness, his ambition and desire drive him to seek that star. To have glimpsed it is to have realized something very real, but beyond possession. Even Sam Gluckman must have been seeking such meaning when he stood for hours in his office watching the eight-foot rings of "simulated cigarette smoke" that issued from the huge tobacco sign in the distance.

To have understood that vision, Keenan insists, is to ask how anyone could have lived his own life differently or how a person could have become other than what he wills himself to be. Since man's nature is to fulfill an inevitable destiny, how, Keenan asks, can destiny possibly keep man from becoming himself. Although he has known pain and suffering and defeat, he sees now that he has been living four of the happiest years of his life.

Only an Inch from Glory tells what happened to some of the "little people" who had, like Halper and his fellow artists, made their way to New York during the 1930's. In the Chicago novels, the little people, for all their poverty and despair, were part of the mainstream of

American life; they were attached by job and place. In these last novels, the characters are rootless and detached; neither their jobs nor their achievements bring more than a small measure of fulfillment. Although money is sometimes their problem, they have more money, a higher standard of living, certainly more talent and sophistication than their "worker" counterparts. But they have achieved no more; their lives are as stereotyped and as desperate.

With its narrow scope, its limited number of characters, its carefully controlled and organized episodes, the novel contains some of Halper's most finished writing. The language, lyrical and rhythmical, but never raw and slangy as in the Chicago novels, has been honed to grammatical perfection. The concentration of events and the skillfully developed web of relationships give it power and intensity. For the first time women play comparable roles to men. In the Chicago novels women have had to cope with a man's world, and while they have served in their usual roles of secretaries, clerks, girl friends, and lovers, they have never occupied more than secondary places. But here Dorothy Lynch takes on an identity of her own; she is the only real heroine in any of Halper's novels. Like the rest of the characters in the novel, she belongs to any era in history which worships false notions and then tries to possess them, and like the world in which she lives, the nature of her character impels her to destruction.

Halper's next novel did not appear until the mid-1950's. *Atlantic Avenue*, published as a 'Dell First Edition' paperback original, takes its title and setting from the avenue in Brooklyn of the same name, a street not unlike the Kedzie Avenue area in Chicago, lined with cheap shops and little "eat" places. Although Atlantic Avenue has its share of honest tradesmen, it is a mecca for shady deals and mysterious connections, a catchall for drunks and loners, for prostitutes and con guys of every nationality. It is a land of losses, but the losses come from gambling and greed and calculated illegal actions, not from poverty and ignorance.

A very short novel, *Atlantic Avenue* is the story of two cousins who came to the Avenue from Istanbul after the war, and of Eileen Feeney who has become involved with both of them. Garo Balik and Nate Abazian represent the double aspect of the Avenue. Garo, slick and handsome, had acquired his tricks of lying and stealing, of dodging blows and foraging as a way of life, long before he came to America at the age of fourteen. Scrapes with the law helped him develop a sixth sense of self-preservation that has already played him false. For robbing a candy store, he served fourteen months in prison. Back on the Avenue, he aims to go "legitimate," but with the opportunity to peddle "hot" merchandise, he compromises his intentions.

By contrast, Nate lives an ordinary life, working as a grocery clerk in Mr. Klaup's Blue Front Store. He saves his money, looks after his canary, hopes to marry Eileen Feeney, who works as a waitress in Goldie's Lunch Room. Mostly a loner, she turns to Nate for money, but easily abandons him when she meets Garo. She has her own code. She refuses a stolen wrist-watch that Garo offers, but she shares his bed with disinterested affection.

Atlantic Avenue threads through their entangling relationships and weaves in a number of sterotyped characters—moronic Artie, who did not talk but took the rap; Ray the Goat, racing expert; small-time businessmen; racketeers and a variety of ethnic workers and hangers-on. The street gives an uncertain unity to the action. Cheap and tawdry like the Avenue, the characters live by their wits; they scheme and connive in pursuit of their dreams and desires, seeking independence and success that seems but parody of the American Dream.

The novel is heavy with plot. Garo violates the rules that his connection with the underworld has given him. The gang seeks revenge. While he evades capture, his escape involves Nate in the whole sordid affair. Nate learns that Eileen has stolen money from her boss, who has committed suicide. He decides to help her instead of Garo. Although the gang still beats him up, Nate does not completely lose hope. Like Garo, he believes they can all start over again.

On Atlantic Avenue nobody really wins. Caught with their dreams and sleazy convictions, they hope to work things out in a honky-tonk world where mere survival is hardly possible for much of the human flotsam and jetsam that make up this part of the city. Is this urban America? Here man's life, seldom bent to his own ideals, is frittered away in shady connections, violent reactions, thoughtless and purposeless acts. The narrative races along with a kind of warm heartedness. The characters live on a simple emotional level; their quirks are seldom funny; their losses and loneliness evoke little sympathy and no admiration. *Atlantic Avenue* is hardly a successful potboiler.

Halper's novel about Miami Beach has little in common with his other writing except his use of the same seedy characters and an urban setting. He had gone to Miami Beach during the summer of 1952, living with a dance team and trying to write an article about them and other Miami dance teams for *The New Yorker*. But the project did not work out. He had put the material aside, and many years later, he used much of it in *The Fourth Horseman of Miami Beach*.

Like *Atlantic Avenue*, *The Fourth Horseman* is a story of violence and family animosity, a tale of man's pursuit of love and sex, of money and property, of leisure and pleasure; but the resolution ends with forgiveness. Halper's narrator plays no part in the action; the plot moves with speed and clarity, and the writing captures some of the slangy rhythms and raucous characterizations of the Chicago novels. The episodes, many of them amusing and intense, describe a nightmare world that the characters accept as ordinary living. Halper's satiric portrayal of the social patterns and personal lives of the "little people" are a clear commentary on the deceptive and fraudulent nature of man as he tries to revenge the passing of youth and cope with the boredom of leisure and retirement.

The scene has an extraordinary effect on the people. As one character says, "Miami Beach ain't a place, it's a frame of mind, a *state* of mind." [3] That state of mind includes sun and ocean, wind and twirling palms, and seasons that melt into a perpetual summer. After coming to Miami Beach, men look on it as an earthly paradise of fun and leisure; they become "obsessed with the belief that they had renewed their youth under this invigorating tropic sun, breathing this balmy sea air. This was an enchanted isle of mirages, delusions" (327–38). But instead of restoring one's youth, the place is fraught with deception and violence, with losers and hangers-on, con men and game sharks, young pimps and prostitutes, with the well-healed and aging "little people" who have retired here for a last fling at the business of living. Drifters, spenders, riffraff, ne'er-do-wells, plain people, they have reduced their lives to an apartment and a deck chair; they huddle together, drinking, gambling, telling stories, seeking protection from the monotony of life and the boredom of living.

One group, the Horsemen, lives at the same hotel. Meeting daily at one o'clock, they subscribe to common aims—"leisurely living, good food, sunshine—and good dames" (121). They depend on each other. As Halper says, "the big ship that had gone down behind them had been their youth." Now they are "floating aimlessly, hoping to reach the safety of some unnamed landfall" (68–69). All three members—the fourth has just died—have been in the clothing business; all of them have a few memories. At age sixty-four, Moe Stein can no longer make love; his daughter, living in California never writes him; after three marriages and three divorces, she has become an alcoholic. Jerry Ryan, a bachelor, has grown "tired from the sun," from the meals he has eaten, from the endless conversations he has had; no one knows of his affair with his business partner's sister that ended in an abortion. Hy Bronson, a salesman in rayons, secretly studies French, because Moe Stein, "green with envy," casts aspersions on Hy's educational background; ill with a kidney problem, he is depressed and lonely. Whatever they have learned has little of the nature of revelation. The new member is more apocalyptic.

Leo Roth, the new fourth Horseman, is still President of the Dilly-Dally Dress Company of New York. He has come to Miami Beach possibly to retire, but mainly to search out his cousin Bernie Flugman, who has embezzled fifteen to twenty thousand dollars of the firm's money, gambled it away, and escaped to Florida. The novel is Leo's story, his search for his cousin, and his escapades with Rosita and Manuel, a dance team whose professional careers and private lives become entangled with his own.

But Leo's real search leads him through a nightmarish world of frustration and revenge and finally brings a revelation of self. He has started as a salesman, worked his way up, only to find that his wife divorces him and exacts a fine settlement. Coming to Miami Beach has brought him neither pleasure nor luck. The woman he picks up is part of a gang that breaks into the hotel room, takes his money, and kicks him out. Realizing what a fool he has been, he stops at a synagogue, but is further embarrassed when he has no money to give the rabbi. Feelings of guilt and insecurity make him wonder if he should forgive his cousin for the theft or exact payment and punishment. A series of happenings help him decide.

As a member of the Horsemen group, Leo quips and banters with them, agrees to pay for the dance lessons that his predecessor has not used, and, in consequence, becomes involved with the most famous dance team at Miami Beach. Manuel and Rosita, tired of New York where they met at a dance contest, came to Miami Beach for the fast buck, lived as if married, and prospered. Manuel, "chaser" of women, is always drifting off; his scheme with Teddy Kirk to buy a sightseeing boat and ply the trade is only a fancy set-up for picking up happy call girls. Even Leo feels the "big ship" of his youth has not completely vanished as Rosita moves in with him. They offer more evidence of the games people play. Marcia Manheim pursues Manuel; Miss Gold and Dottie Kaplan pursue Leo Roth; Rosita merely uses Leo to get back at Manuel. As Leo settles into the Miami Beach pattern, he is satiated with food and sex, but frustrated at not finding his cousin.

Bernie Flugman is not found, but rescued. Unable to win enough to pay off the gang who have followed him to Miami Beach, Bernie is trapped by Galetti's guys, who overhaul him and leave him on the beach as a throwaway. He is discovered and taken to the hospital, where his arrest is an easy matter. But Leo has changed, "his anger somehow had left him." Why? As the narrator explains,

this town has altered [Leo] deeply, irrevocably. His new acquaintances here, the experiences he had had, even the balmy air, had left their marks upon him. And was it not true . . . that in hunting down Bernie, he had, somehow, been searching for something in himself? (322)

In learning forgiveness, Leo has also learned that deception defines much of life, especially in this enchanting and deluding land. Remorse over Dot Kaplan's attempted suicide is hardly justified; she has only used Leo as a blind to avenge a husband who refuses to divorce her, but who is keeping another woman at a nearby hotel. Leo knows now that he can not remain and "watch the bright days wheel by uselessly on a sun deck which sparkled with the ever-present, illusionary, health-tanning sunrays of idleness and approaching old age!" (331). Better keep selling, he concludes, and returns to New York.

One of the best episodes reunites Rosita and Manuel at a dance contest. Their "controlled abandon" identifies their lifestyle. Halper's use of an art form as a way of bringing people together, of channeling violent emotions, of giving shape and understanding to man's thought and feeling recalls a similar use of music in *The Foundry* and *Only an Inch from Glory*. What Leo Roth has gained in self-awareness, others have not. As the three remaining Horsemen drift toward idleness in the futile business of trying to capture the illusion of youth, they spot a new prospect who might join them as a 'fourth.' Such fun and games is their endless hope.

In *The Fourth Horseman of Miami Beach*, it is as if the "little people" of the Chicago novels have grown old and tired. Like the young, they pursue a life of pleasure and sex, or they talk about their past escapades. They hover on the fringes of fear and boredom, chattering away and telling dirty jokes to each other under the guise of leisurely living and happy contentment. They have money; they do not worry about values. In retirement they have become fat and tanned and conspicuously irrelevant. The satiric language, the jokes, the quirks of character offer comment on a world of the 1960's that had not so much crashed, as was simply coming apart.

In the Chicago novels, the characters gained identity through work. In *The Fourth Horseman*, work is mostly incidental to the life of sex and violence that, tangled and frustrated, is seldom resolved. Only Leo Roth possesses a genuinely sympathetic and compassionate attitude; his forgiveness of his cousin is a positive act. His traits, often found in characters of the earlier novels, are realized here through self-achievement. Leo has not only grown in stature; but in learning about self, he has also comprehended a revelation befitting a fourth Horseman.

The Fourth Horseman of Miami Beach has more action than depth, more sensationalism than real insight. Like a fast stepping revue, the story, mostly fun and games, forms an amusing epilogue to the novels of the 1930's.

II   *Chicago Revisited:*   The Golden Watch

After World War II, Halper's productivity began to decrease. Although he had always written about the people he knew—and there was plenty of material among his bohemian friends in New York—he had frequently returned to his early life for subject material. As he said, Chicago had remained his literary and spiritual home. By the early 1950's, he had accumulated a number of stories that he had written between the years 1936 and 1951 about his family and about his growing up on Chicago's West Side. Using a plan similar to that of *On the Shore*, he assembled fifteen related stories about his past, twelve of which had already appeared in magazines. He made but few changes, revising introductory sentences where needed and making the names of the narrator's family consistent throughout. Dedicating the collection to his son Tommy, who had been born in 1942, he published *The Golden Watch*, his second volume of short stories, in 1953.

The Golden Watch proposes no new themes, in a sense covers no new material, but simply adds other "chapters" to his West Side saga. The stories follow a chronological pattern; the first one begins with the narrator's eighth year; the last one tells of his graduation from high school, when he receives a gold Elgin pocket watch as a gift from his family. Both the watch and the graduation mark a turning point in the boy's life.

Each story is presented as an episode that instructs the narrator in moral thought and social behavior. The teller is both observer and participant in most of the events, and as he learns about others, about man's dreams and failures, his pride and illusions, his frauds and deceits, his capacities for love and understanding, about the ironies of circumstance and the quirks of fate, so he learns about himself. Some of these events are public ceremony as well as private happening. At the Passover celebration in "Warm Matzos," Milt, the eldest son, leaves before the ceremony has ended. For the first time, the narrator feels a loneliness that indicates how the family unity is breaking up. At the graduation ceremonies in the final episode, when the gold watch is presented to the narrator, the watch becomes both a gift and a memento, a symbol of time that marks the moment of ending and beginning that graduation suggests. For his mother and father, the watch, like time, has different meanings—mother, sensing time's swift passage, avoids thinking of it; father, having converted time into achievement, declares that he is the "only one here with real experience in life. . . . Don't listen to any heavy nonsense. Life will be your advice. . . ." [4] For the narrator, his father's advice becomes a course of action; for Halper the writer, it becomes the basis of his writing career.

Most of the stories deal with minor incidents that, nonetheless, show how a young and sensitive mind grasps meaning and gathers ideas. He is given a lesson in independence by brother Milt's confidence and success, for as a traveling salesman, Milt breaks away from family patterns of conduct and follows his own thinking; in deception, as brother Ben reveals their arrogant cousin Sam to be "only a run-of-the-mill drummer, after all . . ." (180); in sacrifice, when Ben gives up a paying job to study medicine and thus becomes the "greatest figure in our world" (185); in belief, when he hears the "prophet" tell the women what wonderful things their children are going to be and then learns that the man has really escaped from a mental institution; or in integrity, as he tries to understand Uncle Tutti's love for "enduring and beautiful things" in a crass and ugly world. As his father tells the narrator, "Life is serious. . . . The young don't grow up by themselves" (203).

More than any other character, father plays a formative role in the narrator's life. Father's candid remarks, his bluster and pride, his wisdom and compassion give an unlooked for insight, a lasting impression. Is it not false pride for father to insist that his problem with eyesight comes from the newspaper's use of smaller type? Is it not deception for Uncle Harry to substitute a new kite for the broken one so that father believes he has punished the boys unjustly for flying their kites in forbidden places? Is father not right about poets living in little rooms and starving to death? This poet does, and the truth has little romance about it. Mother's influence, less apparent, helps clarify the narrator's awareness of change. When sister Ruth arrives home from her first date, mother understands a need for tolerance, while father only blusters. As the insights accumulate, so the narrator develops his own thoughts and notions that signify his real graduation.

Episodes in *The Golden Watch* have the quaint look of "urban" pastoral; with their air of innocence and nostalgia and gentle humor, the stories have, as Nelson Algren writes, "the unpretentiousness and the unaffected warmth of Chekhov, while lacking only Chekhov's edge of iron." [5] Written with affection and authority, the stories are less concerned with the fads and fashions of an era than with the perennial problems of youth and the process of growing up and trying to understand human behavior. Halper catches a quality of life that is both timely and timeless. As Algren writes, "so gently are these stories told, so softly illuminated, that it is hard to realize all this happened only yesterday. It seems another land." [6] *The Golden Watch* contains some of Halper's best writing. What he said of his Indian friend at the post office applies to his own work—the talk is straight and strong; the thinking, direct and clear.

III   *Chicago Revisited: The Anthologies*

Halper's travel essay on Chicago in 1951, his nonpolitical analysis of the city as "capital of conventioneers" in 1952, and the prefatory material in the two anthologies about the city celebrate Chicago with much the same affection and admiration found in the novels and short stories, except that here he is more factual and more explicitly autobiographical.

This is Chicago, An Anthology, appeared in 1952; Halper had purposely compiled it from "Chicagoans and non-Chicagoans alike." As editor, he set about "painting an honest, sensitive, and extremely 'viewable' portrait of a huge city that has always been exciting and newsworthy nationally and internationally." He wanted, he wrote, to present the city's past and present, its changing moods, its infinite variety. As he said, "Chicago is not only a city, it is a city of cities— made up of great foreign blocs of population, impinging on one another." [7] Both the introduction and the prefatory notes to each selection attest Halper's warmth and compassion for the people and events that have given the city some of its unique character.

The selections include both factual reports of public events and fictional stories of personal happenings; as Halper believes, they not only tell the social and inner history of Chicago, but they also tell the social and inner history of all America—the nomination of Abraham Lincoln as President of the United States, the Haymarket Affair, the great Chicago fire, the Columbian Exposition of 1893, the second Tunney-Dempsey fight, the Loeb-Leopold case, Jane Addams' work at Hull House. In turn, such writers as Carl Sandburg, Sherwood Anderson, Edna Ferber, Richard Wright, Nelson Algren, James T. Farrell, Gwendolyn Brooks, and others have revealed Chicago to the world with a forthrightness and an inner honesty that describe both their writings and the city itself. As Halper says, revealing something of his own style when he says it, a "finely mannered Chicago writer is almost unthinkable." The anthology is like a scrapbook of Halper's own memories.

A second anthology, *The Chicago Crime Book*, was published in 1967. Although the twenty-four selections deal specifically with crime in Chicago, they also tell the more inclusive story of one of America's foremost domestic problems and thus are "to be read as pressing history on a national scale." [8] Chicago, Halper writes, never a "pseudo-European" city like New York, Boston, or Philadelphia, may well stand for "the true ethos of our national landscape." In its successful pursuit of crime, the city is simply representative of all America.

In preparing the volume, Halper returned to Chicago, searching carefully for material in libraries, newspaper reference rooms, and photo morgues. In assembling the volume, he arranged the stories in three sections: those of the era of Al Capone; those that tell of the "city's spectacular murders of a nongangster nature," such as the Loeb-Leopold case, the Holmes-Castle case, the Degnan murder case; and those of the presently entrenched Syndicate, which threaten our present "existence as we go to the supermarket, buy gasoline, take our clothes to the cleaners, or visit a nightclub." [9] Most of the writers, probably less known than the gangsters they write about, are newspaper men; Halper pays tribute to them as having contributed "among the true folk tales of our time." [10]

IV   *Chicago Revisited: Theater*

Halper's success in the theater has been limited, but in *My Aunt Daisy*, based on his own short story, which he and Joseph Schrank adapted for the stage, he returns once more to his Chicago past. Set in a walk-up flat over a small grocery store, the script sticks close to Halper's story of a silly New England nymphomaniac, who visits her relatives in Chicago and has a little affair with a "portly suitor" from a nearby railroad roundhouse. In its short run at the Westport Country Playhouse (Westport, Connecticut) in August, 1954, Jo Van Fleet played the central role. In November, 1955, *Top Man*, the story of a doctor "whose early promise has been dissipated by repeated irregularities in his professional and private life," opened in New Haven, Connecticut, and closed in Philadelphia, after a short run. Although the cast included Polly Bergen, Ralph Meeker, Lee Remick, and Heywood Hale Broun, the play never reached Broadway.[11]

V   A Writer Remembering

Halper had been writing about his family and friends and about himself from the beginning of his career, but in *Good-Bye, Union Square, A Writer's Memories of the Thirties* (1970), he gives his own nonfictional account of the young writer who came to New York and found that his memories of Chicago, not his new found friends in New York, made staying there as a writer worth while. A loner, not a joiner, he brought with him an independence of thought, an integrity of belief, and the self-determination to succeed as a writer.

As he settled down in shabby rooms and unfurnished apartments with his typewriter and a bare light bulb, he wrote about the only world he knew—his own. Since he had been a worker and knew about work and working conditions, he seemed all the more vulnerable to entreaties of friends, editors, and believers who insisted that he join the Communist Party and help promote the goals and aims of the revolutionaries. But he wanted to write, not reform people, and he wanted to write about individuals that he knew and had observed, not about political causes and revolutionary tactics. When he finally settled near Union Square, he did so because rents were cheap and because he wanted to remain independent and to work alone.

Yet as a writer of social criticism at a time when the mainstream of American thought was seeking an understanding of depressed social and economic conditions, Halper might well have joined causes and organizations that were both opportune and fashionable. He did not. Although he published in such liberal and left-wing magazines as the *New Republic, Partisan Review*, and *New Masses*, he had never been a member of the John Reed Club, the Communist Party, or other communist-front organizations. He had no reason to suspect that he would ever be subject to investigation for left-wing activities and espionage. Yet he was. His suspected involvement and subsequent questioning by the FBI provide the central episode and framework for *Good-bye, Union Square*. Reflection on the episode, in turn, releases a flood of memories that recalls the story of his coming to New York to write—and of his literary agent, who entrapped him in an espionage plot. The story, not revealed until the book's publication in 1970, has all the ingredients of a nightmare.

In early August, 1948, shortly after Whittaker Chambers had accused Alger Hiss of communist connections, the Federal Bureau of Investigation visited Halper to ask him to identify his own signature, which they had found on a document in their possession. The name Albert Halper appeared as the fourth officer on the incorporation papers of the American Feature Writers Syndicate, an espionage cover organization that listed its address as that of Max Lieber, Halper's agent. Halper readily agreed that the signature was his, but he could not remember signing this particular document. He did recall that Lieber himself had been a communist, and he had uncertain knowledge that Lieber had used the agency as a guise for communist activities. He also remembered that Lieber had sometimes asked him to sign as a witness for literary contracts, which he had done, sometimes without reading them thoroughly or at all. He had signed this document without reading it, assuming that he was serving in the same capacity. With the assurance that his agent's duplicity was firmly established, Halper first confronted Lieber, who refused to discuss it, and then severed all ties with him.

The agency quickly fell apart. Lieber had already suffered a heart attack before the investigations started. When the Hiss-Chambers trial ended, he left New York, suffered another heart attack, and finally escaped to Mexico and then to Poland, where he worked in a State publishing house. When he returned to America on business in the mid-1960's, he telephoned Halper. Halper said the call "had peeled away the years. . . ." [12] What he remembers of the young writer coming to New York and living near Union Square is part of the literary history of an era.

Good-bye, Union Square tells the personal story of a writer who set about trying to understand the "buried" years of a "person," as he referred to himself, "who has truly lived and loved in New York during the 1930's." [13] As writer, Halper had belonged to that era as to no other, and because he had grown up in an urban world, had worked in it before he tried to write about it, and had remembered it with a fine objectivity, he came to understand the people who work in the city better than most writers. Once in his youth, walking along the railroad tracks, he remembers hearing the train coming. He stepped aside and waited: "it whirled past me, shot round the curve and went out of sight, but I still hear it yet." [14] And so, I think, can the reader.

CHAPTER 8

Good-bye, Again: In Conclusion

THE writings of Albert Halper are inextricably linked with Chicago, with the 1930's, with the people who came to make up his own private world of memories. Although the characters in his stories and novels, many of them modeled on his family and on the workers whom he had known, have aspirations and desires, Halper is neither a sentimentalist nor a visionary. His writing is informed with the energy and spirit of his Jewish immigrant family, with their dreams of independence and self-reliance, and with their honesty and capacity for work.

His formative years were shaped, as he has said, by growing up on Chicago's West Side. As an individual, he grew sensitive to the ironies of living, to the natural world of the Windy City that seeped into his life as wind and sun and the lake's shore. As a worker and finally as a writer, he observed the quirks and foibles of people, listened to their stories, witnessed the patterns of their response, their frustrations and loneliness, their tedium and despair, the hopelessness of working all day at a monotonous job and returning at night to the agony of fading dreams, the losses that come with man's ignorance, his inertia, his inability to get the breaks that seldom come.

Although he began to write at a time when social problems and radical causes were stirring literary traditions, he became neither propagandist nor reformer. For him writing was always a personal proposition; he wrote about those who irritated him, about the people he knew, about his own experiences, about the friction between character and idea, but he saw an individual's experiences as taking place always within a larger social and economic context, just as he saw individuals contending with moral values that sometimes frustrated their lives and left them lonely and afraid. Although Halper penetrated the facade of society and looked at the personal lives of people, he seldom probes deeply into motives or the dark corners of mental disturbance or analyzes sociological and psychological causes and effects. His understanding of man's condition and of man's inner world is revealed, rather, through a minute description of behaviorial patterns, of the relation of individuals to each other and to their jobs.

Like many of the artists whom he admired—Mark Twain and Theodore Dreiser, James Joyce and Sherwood Anderson, Pieter Breughel and Hieronymus Bosch, Anton Chekhov and Nikolai Gogol—he tried to depict life with an abiding honesty that had little to do with such literary labels as realism, naturalism, and proletarianism. As a writer, he thought of himself as a commentator or a historian; thus writing for him became a recollection of things past, the memories of people and places.

As the young writer in New York remembering Chicago or the mature writer bidding good-bye to Union Square, he focused mainly on the narrow segment of city life that he had known, although it limited his range more than his depth of insight. He knew what it was to grow up in a dreary section of a large city, to work endless hours in factory or store, to live in poverty and loneliness and dream of being a writer. What makes Halper's work a significant achievement in American letters, Freeman Champney rightly declared in 1942, was his ability to portray "the feel of what life means to most urban Americans." [1] He knew the city, its streets, its tempo, its violence, its competition and struggle, its capacities for sympathy, compassion, even forgiveness.

As historian of those who earn their daily bread in "factories, stores, and offices," Halper writes of people and places in terms of a collectivity, though he is little concerned with collective action or collective solutions. A few characters, like Karl Heitman in *The Foundry*, or Fuerstein in *The Chute*, even Jason Wheeler in *Union Square*, are reformers with a cause, but the bulk of Halper's people simply struggle along, pursuing their daily jobs. In time, many of them run headlong into social issues, engage in strikes, shout Marxian slogans, follow the path of expediency, of sudden notion or desire, but they know little of the mysteries of economics, the complexities of power.

What they do know of the "social and economic conditions" is determined mostly on a personal level. As Halper had learned, workers take their identity from their jobs, from their special skills, from the factory or company or street that they know. Life is lived on a personal level—the fear that a dismissal notice brings for worker and family; the rejection of a painting or story that shatters a man's hopes; the strike or work slowdown that may mean social gain, but always means loss of pay; the effect of speed on a man's legs and feet and nerves and digestion; the defeats and frustrations of a love affair; the loss of moral values to the demands and needs of desire and passion; the hypocrisy of those who change their attitudes and notions to fit a temporary convenience. Halper's real concern is with individuals, with their relation to place and groups, with their hopes and despairs, their honesty and integrity, their ignorance and forbearance.

Yet man's personal problems are also the social and economic problems of an era: personal injustices become unfair labor practices, the idiocy and chicanery of conniving bosses, the failure, even, of businesses and established leadership. As his writing builds on auto-biography, so his portrayal of individuals, provincial and repetitious, takes on a deeper meaning, applicable to industrial and urban life everywhere. Arranged in sequence, his stories and novels constitute not only a history of his own life, but also a social commentary on an era. What emerges is not an analysis of class conflict or the failure of economic and political systems, but an exposition of the meanness, the drabness of people's lives, the sheer waste and exploitation of human effort, the incompetence and trickery of free-style individual-ism, the decay of moral values, the empty lives of little people. While such problems are deeply enmeshed in the social and economic fabric of a society, their consequences are not easily solved or quickly changed.

But in writing about individuals, Halper's concerns are neither with victories nor with heroics. He proffers no certain solutions, only ironic endings. Many characters follow a pattern of adventure that has all the possibilities for self-achievement. They venture forth into the unknown world of dirty streets, of speed and noise, of endless belts and whirling cogs, into the maze of aisles and counters, into an industrial or urban jungle, or into the illusory world of Miami Beach. But their adventures, ordinary, petty, real, are just as agonizing and demanding of mind and body and spirit as a more romantic venture in a more exotic place. Sometimes a character does achieve, but the achievement is mild and minor, the little insight, the sudden aware-ness that results, perhaps, in a change of direction, a minimal growth. August Kafka in *The Foundry* composes a symphony that unites the factory audience for a brief insight; Paul Sussman, having escaped the mail-order house jungle, now has hopes of studying architecture; Oscar Bresslin in *The Little People* gives Helen Browning the com-passion she has so unhappily earned. Frank Keenan in *Only an Inch from Glory* and Leo Roth in *The Fourth Horseman* are loosely guided by moral and religious values that enable them to clarify their experience and deepen their insight; both of them achieve an understanding and a compassion or, at least, return to a sanity that has long eluded them.

Much of the vividness of Halper's writing derives from his portrayal of characters. They are meticulously described in endless eye-witness detail by the omniscient narrator. In the Chicago novels more than in the later ones, Halper invariably creates characters with identifying quirks and mannerisms. In *The Chute* Big Bill Dorpat, late of Amsterdam, retains his thick accent; Boswell in *The Foundry* has a song for every occasion. The bosses in *The Foundry* and *The Little People* have an assortment of illnesses. In nearly every novel— Pinky and Jack Duffy in *The Foundry*, Joey Applebaum in *The Chute*, Al Grimes in *The Little People*, Moe Stein in *The Fourth Horseman*, Old Bromovitch in *Sons of the Fathers*—a character resorts to fancy talk, speaking in a kind of "fantastic, mock-grandiloquent fashion" of assorted slang and slogans, the high-blown oratory and endless joking that both identifies their personalities and reveals their inner thoughts and motivation. Critics dismiss this distinctive and imaginative flair as unsound practice, but the characters exhibit vitality and identity through Halper's descriptive language and speech.

Perhaps the essential vigor of Halper's writing lies in his use of language. Sometimes ungrammatical, sometimes barbaric, his sentences rush and flow in a racy stream; his language seems admirably suited to his characters and to his subject material. Freeman Champney correctly observes that Halper's language is that

of the imaginative, half-cocky, half-cynical young man of working-class Chicago. It bears the marks of self-education: of the deposit of many scraps and fragments of haphazard reading, of vitality beaten down and kicked around but not defeated, of Jewish, Polish, German, Slovenian, and numerous other half-assimilated language and culture groups.[2]

Especially in the novels, Halper's sentences are boldly assertive, frequently exclamatory, swinging along with a directness and vivacity that preclude subtlety of phrasing and idea. The sentences, thick with metaphor, often not very original, are lyrical and poetic, clicking along with a heady exhilaration. The stories move at a slower pace, exhibiting an innocence and an irony which reflect a pre-World War I era, and contrast stoutly with the urban world of the novels.

What reviewers and critics denigrated as skillful reporting and clever manipulation of conventional material was, then, as Halper saw it, an honest search for the proper form to express his vision of the world he had experienced. As he wrote in discussing *Windy City Blues*, his second unpublished novel, it might have been readily accepted if he had written it in "straight prose, no interludes etc." As he said, he thought it as "one of the few attempts at real twangy American writing, with slang and the tempo of American speech thrown in." [3] The aim he expresses here also describes his aim in the other novels. His attention to sentence structure and speech rhythms; his use of poetic prose passages such as those in *Union Square* or "Young Writer Remembering Chicago"; his episodic development of plot that has become now fashionable in the 1970's; his use of a vast number of characters; all attest his sensitivity to the fragmented attitudes and broken patterns of modern life, to the need for expressing that drift and tempo in a loose and flexible form. In using the episodic form of the "revue," he was able to frame his material with the collective patterns of job or street and at the same time present a series of related skits that would catch the inner thoughts and feelings of individuals.

Halper's use of a less conventional form of the novel did not mar the vigor of his language, his accurate observation of the actions and peculiarities of individuals, his naive and earthy sensitivity to nature and to changes in the world around him. Nor did it impede his capacity as story-teller; at his best his insights into the foibles and habits of people are quickly humorous and ironically penetrating. Never the aspiring Marxian or proletarian propagandist that many called him, he was consciously the artist, consciously the student of human nature, intent on exploring broad social problems and presenting moral issues. As worker and writer, he had an immense compassion and sympathy for the "underdog," for the ignorances and shortcomings of little people, for their whims and endless longings. His vivid and forceful picture of how such people lived and thought and felt is also a vivid picture of the people of all America in the 1930's.

"As the years go by," Halper writes in *Good-bye, Union Square*, ". . . one begins to hope that if one's own writing has been good, perhaps one's contribution during the thirties will one day find its way into the flow of the mainstream." [4] The 1930's had been, he thought, "perhaps the most vital part" of his work. Although the era had defined and limited his direction, his subject material had the appeal of history and the delight of the story-teller's art. He had shown us the conditions of life, how man had endured guilt and fear and hope and despair, yet had somehow learned to endure and forgive. However fragile and fleeting such values may seem, they have fortified man against a hostile and violently changing world.

Halper's best writing falls within a period from 1933 to 1943. His Chicago novels and stories are literally sandwiched between the two novels about New York. As it is, *Union Square* begins with a riot; *Only an Inch from Glory* ends with death and violence. But the Chicago stories, which contain his best work, dramatize the moral, social, and economic conflicts of that stormy era. In retrospect *Union Square*, his best-known novel, remains a tour de force, heavy with irony and stock characters; yet in depicting the events of the Square in a lyrical and twangy language, he succeeds in showing how man lived in that sodden world of the Depression. *Only an Inch from Glory*, succinctly written and carefully organized, shows how bohemians and artists fared in their conquest of the city during wartime.

But his abilities are best displayed in *The Chute* and *The Little People*. Here the authenticity of his own perceptions and feelings has shaped the remembered events and recreated his experiences into a coherent and forceful statement about man's struggle with a world of speed and noise, of deceit and frustration and dishonesty. Here his use of the changing seasons, integral to the economics of business and to the feelings of workers, becomes an allegory of progress that combines with a single symbol of horrendous destruction and hopeful change. Although the clash of human will against mechanized power is more nakedly obvious in *The Foundry*, the same conflict, clearly explicit in *The Chute* and *The Little People*, makes those novels unique achievements in showing how it felt to live and work in urban and industrial America. Many of the stories about Chicago's West Side capture this same remembered frustration. "Young Writer Remembering Chicago" is a small classic that gives a more egocentric picture of Halper's own life in an urban world. *The Golden Watch* presents some of the best vignettes of his father, who appears in most of the Chicago stories and novels, and whose dominant and determined character supplies touchstones of moral measurement for a world filled with hypocrisy and greed and false notions. Through his father's character, Halper declares his own sympathy for those who deserve a gentle and sometimes hard-earned forgiveness. There are no winners; there are few losers. The best, like his father, simply watch and wait and endure.

Halper's wish to become part of the mainstream of American letters sounds a note of faith and belief that characterizes the independent spirit of his writing, for he follows in the tradition of Emerson and Twain, of Stephen Crane and Sinclair Lewis, of Sherwood Anderson and the early Hemingway. He has deserved better treatment than time and critical neglect have given him. A talented writer in a decade that produced few major writers, he has remembered well the raw and changing world of his Chicago days with joy and humor and a kind of cosmic laughter. Like all sentient beings, he has had an abiding appreciation for the natural world, a feeling for wind and rain and sun and endless change. These memories still tell us about our past, about ourselves, and about America.

Notes and References

Chapter One

1. Albert Halper, *This Is Chicago* (New York, 1952), p. viii.
2. Albert Halper, "It's the Giant of America's Heartland," *Holiday*, X (October, 1951), 45 and 54. Hereafter cited as "Giant."
3. Dale Kramer, *Chicago Renaissance* (New York, 1966), p. 346.
4. *This Is Chicago*, p. viii.
5. "A Herring for My Uncle," *The American Mercury*, XXVII (November, 1932), 367.
6. "Dynamic Capital of Conventioneers," *The New York Times Magazine*, June 29, 1952, p. 36. Hereafter cited as "Dynamic Capital."
7. "Giant," p. 47.
8. "Dynamic Capital," p. 36.
9. "Giant," p. 47.
10. "Giant," p. 47.
11. "Giant," p. 51.
12. Albert Halper, "The Poet," *The Virginia Quarterly Review*, XII (April, 1936), 248.
13. Albert Halper, "Young Writer, Remembering Chicago," *The Menorah Journal*, XIX (November–December, 1930), 147.
14. Albert Halper, "Hot Night on the West Side," *On the Shore* (New York, 1934), p. 168.
15. Albert Halper, *The Chicago Crime Book* (Cleveland, 1967), p. 385.
16. *This Is Chicago*, p. 88.
17. Albert Halper, *Good-bye, Union Square* (Chicago, 1970), p. 30. Philipsborn was taken over by Spiegel, May, Stern, and Company, which still exists as Spiegel, Inc.
18. Albert Halper, "A Song Writer in the Family," *The Yale Review*, XXXIII (December, 1944), 258.
19. "Spectator," *Wings: The Literary Guild Magazine*, VII (March, 1933), 13. Edited by Harriet Colby, *Wings* was published monthly by the Literary Guild and was intended for circulation only among Guild members.
20. *Good-bye, Union Square*, p. 149.
21. Albert Halper, *Purple Pudding* (Chicago, 1927), p. 2.
22. *Good-bye, Union Square*, p. 232.

23. Halper's statements in *Twentieth Century Authors*, edited by Stanley J. Kunitz and Howard Haycraft (1942), p. 603.

24. Albert Halper, "The Plight of the Postal Subs," *New Masses*, XII (July 31, 1934), 18.

25. Albert Halper, "Chicago Mail Clerks," *The Debunker*, IX (February, 1929), 5.

26. Ibid.

27. In *Twentieth Century Authors*, p. 603.

28. "Giant," p. 48.

29. In *Twentieth Century Authors*, p. 603.

Chapter Two

1. In *Twentieth Century Authors*, p. 604.

2. *Good-bye, Union Square*, pp. 26–31.

3. Ibid., p. 49.

4. Ibid.

5. *Good-bye, Union Square*, pp. 32–33. Fyodor Sologub, the pseudonym of Fyodor Kuzmich Teternikov (1863–1927), was a Russian poet and prose writer. His prose masterpiece, *The Little Demon* (1916), is a satiric and symbolic story of a petty and base hero. Aleksei Mikhailovich Remizov (1877–1957), Russian poet and novelist, wrote *The Pond* in 1907, which describes the author's revulsion to city life. Ivan Sergeyevich Turgenev (1813–1883), Russian dramatist, short-story writer, and novelist is best known for his masterpiece *Fathers and Sons* (1862). Pio Baroja y Nessi (1872–1956), Spanish novelist, wrote over eighty titles, including a dozen volumes of essays; portrayed the Madrid underworld in *The Quest*, 1921; *Weeds*, 1923; *Red Dawn*, 1924. Mikhail Yurevich Lermontov (1814–1841), Russian poet, admired Byron, Schiller, and Heine. His novels include *A Hero of Our Times*, 1840. Thomas Mann (1875–1955), German novelist, wrote *Buddenbrooks* (1913), *Death in Venice* (1911), *The Magic Mountain* (1924), and others.

6. *Good-bye, Union Square*, p. 33.

7. Ibid., p. 117.

8. Ibid., p. 80.

9. *This Is Chicago*, p. 305.

10. Ibid., p. 294.

11. Ibid., p. 1.

12. Ibid., p. 30.

13. *Good-bye, Union Square*, p. 28.

14. "Whites Writing Up the Blacks," *The Dial*, LXXXVI (January, 1929), 29. Later, in *Good-bye, Union Square*, Halper devotes a chapter to "Three Black Writers," including Claude McKay, Langston Hughes, and Richard Wright. He thought that *Native Son* was a landmark and that both it and *Black Boy* deserved the literary fame each had received.

15. Ibid., p. 30.

16. "White Laughter," *On the Shore*, pp. 198–99. The six pieces on the post office include "Chicago Mail Clerks," 1929; "On the Shore," 1929; "Payday on the Night Shift," 1931; "White Laughter," 1931; "The Feud in the Rotunda," 1933; "The Plight of the Postal Subs," 1934.

17. "On the Shore," *The Dial*, LXXXVI (January, 1929), 227.

18. Ibid., p. 228.

19. Ibid.

20. *Good-bye, Union Square*, p. 24.

21. "Brothers Over a Grave," *The Menorah Journal*, XVI (April, 1929), 367.

22. "Memorial," *The Menorah Journal*, XVIII (May, 1930), 463–64.

23. "Young Writer, Remembering Chicago," *The Menorah Journal*, XIX (November–December, 1930), 157.

24. *Good-bye, Union Square*, p. 62.

25. Ibid., p. 88.

26. "A Farewell to the Rising Son," *Pagany*, II (April–June, 1931), 1. Hereafter cited as "Farewell."

27. "Farewell," pp. 1 and 6.

28. "Farewell," p. 12.

29. "Farewell," II (October–December), 129.

30. "Farewell," p. 132.

31. "Notes on Novel Writing," *The Writer*, LVII (August, 1944), 227.

32. Ibid., p. 228.

33. "Notes on Jewish-American Fiction," *The Menorah Journal*, XX (April–June, 1932), 63–64.

34. "Notes on Novel Writing," p. 227.

35. "Under Forty," *Contemporary Jewish Record*, VII (February, 1944), 23.

36. "Notes on Jewish-American Fiction," p. 62.

37. Ibid., p. 64.

38. Ibid., pp. 62–63.

39. Ibid., pp. 66–67.

40. Ibid., p. 63.

41. "Under Forty," pp. 24–25.

42. "How to Write Realistic Stories," *The Writer*, LIX (March 1946), 74.

43. *Good-bye, Union Square*, p. 130.

Chapter Three

1. Albert Halper, Letter to Marshall Best, April 20, 1931. In *Good-bye, Union Square*, Halper recalls that during the year following his return from Europe (1935–36), he had felt too stale to do much work. The editors at Viking Press (including Marshall Best) urged him to revise *Windy City Blues* and even drew up a contract. Halper reread the manuscript, but immediately

withdrew. As he said, it should "have been published as a first novel several years ago, not now." See p. 234.

2. Albert Halper, "Behind the Scenes of Union Square," *Wings: The Literary Guild Magazine*, VII (March, 1933), 8. Hereafter cited as "Behind the Scenes."

3. "Behind the Scenes," p. 8.

4. Leonard Q. Ross, *The Strangest Places* (New York, 1939) p. 65.

5. Edmund Wilson, *The Shores of Light* (New York, 1952, 1961) pp. 525–26.

6. *Good-bye, Union Square*, p. 127.

7. "Behind the Scenes," p. 5.

8. *Good-bye, Union Square*, p. 128.

9. "Behind the Scenes," p. 5.

10. Albert Halper, *Union Square* (New York, 1933), pp. 50–51. Subsequent references will appear in the text. Artist Lynd Ward's illustrations provided End Papers for the volume.

11. William Soskin, "Reading and Writing," New York *Evening Post*, Monday, March 6, 1933, p. 9. col. 1.

12. John Chamberlain, "Union Square on and Off the Soap Box," *The New York Times Book Review*, Sunday, March 5, 1933, Section 6, p. 6.

13. G. R. B. R., "Realism as Applied to Seething Life in New York," Boston *Evening Transcript*, Wednesday, April 5, 1933, Part 4, p. 2, col. 5.

14. Carl Van Doren, "*Union Square*," *Wings: The Literary Guild Magazine*, VII (March, 1933), 10–11.

15. Isidor Schneider, "Rain in Union Square," *The Nation*, CXXXVI (April 26, 1933), 478–79.

16. Robert Cantwell, "Four Novelists of Tomorrow," *The New Republic*, LXXIV (March 8, 1933), 108–09. An imperceptive review that also discusses James T. Farrell's *Gas-House McGinty*, Meyer Levin's *The New Bridge*, and Marjorie Kinnan Rawlings' *South Moon Under*.

17. Michael Gold, "Stale Bohemianism," *New Masses*, VIII (April, 1933), 29–30. Also see: G. R. Leighton, "Brought to Life," *The Saturday Review of Literature*, IX (March 4, 1933), 465; Florence Loeb Kellogg, "Folks Around the Square," *Survey Graphic*, XXII (June, 1933), 330; E. B. C. Jones, "New Novels," *The New Statesman and Nation*, VI (July 29, 1933), 136–37; Louise Maunsell Field, "American Novelists vs. the Nation," *The North American Review*, CCXXXV (June, 1933), 552–60.

Chapter Four

1. *Good-bye, Union Square*, p. 8.

2. *This Is Chicago*, p. v.

3. *On the Shore* (New York, 1934), p. 136. Subsequent references will appear in the text.

4. Harold Strauss, "Albert Halper's Boyhood," *The New York Times Book Review*, February 25 (Sunday), 1934, Section 5, p. 11.

5. Alvah Bessie, "Chicago's West Side," *The Saturday Review of Literature*, X (March 10, 1934), 538.

6. Robert Coates, "Five New Novels," *The New Republic*, LXXVIII (March 28, 1934), p. 190–91.

7. Horace Gregory, "Without Money in Chicago," New York *Herald Tribune Books*, Sunday, February 18, 1934, Section VII, p. 2.

8. Wallace Phelps. "New Sketches of Chicago by the Author of 'Union Square,' " (New York) *Daily Worker*, Saturday, March 31, 1934, p. 7, cols 3 and 4.

9. Norman Macleod, "With Malice Towards None," *New Masses*, XI (May 1, 1934), 24–25. Phelps had defended Mike Gold's "harsh criticism" of *Union Square*, but Macleod declared that Gold "did not even give it a review by any sort of standard whatsoever. He spat on it." He thought that *Union Square* was "accurate enough" as far as it went. The Communist simply wanted Halper to join the Party and follow the prescribed line.

10. *Good-bye, Union Square*, pp. 87–88.

11. Floyd Dell, "Three Leaders of Revolt," *The Liberator*, II (July, 1919), 49. Review of a novel about the IWW by Harold Lord Varney entitled *Revolt*.

12. *Good-bye, Union Square*, p. 88.

13. Albert Halper, in "Correspondence" 'The Only Way Out' (a letter) *New Masses*, X (February 27, 1934), 24.

14. See Daniel Aaron, *Writers on the Left* (New York, 1961), p. 270.

15. Albert Halper, "Change the World" (column), *Daily Worker*, June 26, 1934, page 5, cols. 1 and 2.

16. Joseph Freeman, "Ivory Towers—White and Red," *New Masses*, XII (September 11, 1934), 20.

17. Ibid., p. 23.

18. Ibid., p. 24.

19. Ibid., p. 22.

20. Leslie Fiedler, *No! In Thunder* (London, 1963), p. 164. Originally a review of *Part of Our Time* by Murray Kempton; now called "The Search for the Thirties."

21. *Good-bye, Union Square*, p. 138

22. Ibid., pp. 150–51.

23. Albert Halper, Letter to Marshall Best, November 15, 1933.

24. Albert Halper, Letter to Marshall Best, February 27, 1934.

25. Albert Halper, Letter to David Zablodowsky, July 9, 1934.

26. Albert Halper, *The Foundry* (New York, 1934), n. p. Subsequent references will appear in the text.

27. Sinclair Lewis, "Blowing Loud Bugles for Albert Halper," New York *Herald Tribune Books*, Sunday, September 9, 1934, Section VII, p. 1.

28. Peter Quennell, (composite review of six recent novels) *The New Statesman and Nation*, VIII (November 10, 1934), 690.

29. Lewis Gannett, "Books and Things," New York *Herald Tribune*, Wednesday, September 5, 1934, p. 17, col. 1.

30. James Burnham, "Proletarian 'Grand Hotel'," *The Nation*, CXXXIX (September 12, 1934), 306.

31. Alvah C. Bessie, "Men and the Machine," *The Saturday Review of Literature*, XI (September 8, 1934), 96.

32. Joseph North, "Still on the Fence," *New Masses*, XII (September 8, 1934), 25.

33. Ibid., p. 24.

34. Ibid. Also see these evaluations: Morley Callaghan in *The Atlantic Monthly*, CLIV (November, 1934), 12 and 14; Mary Colum in *The Forum*, XCII (November, 1934), 276–80; C. Hartley Grattan in *The Modern Monthly*, VIII (September, 1934), 504–05.

Chapter Five

1. *Good-bye, Union Square*, p. 195.

2. Malcolm Cowley, *Exile's Return* (New York, 1934), p. 300.

3. Jack Conroy, "Robert Cantwell's *Land of Plenty*," in *Proletarian Writers of the Thirties*, edited by David Madden with a preface by Harry T. Moore (Carbondale and Edwardsville, 1968), p. 74.

4. Alfred Kazin, *Starting Out in the Thirties* (New York, 1962, 1965), p. 13.

5. Albert Halper, *The Chute* (New York, 1937), pp. 16–17. Subsequent references will appear in the text.

6. *The Chute* received fewer, briefer, but better reviews than *The Foundry* and *Union Square*. Those referred to here include: Fanny Butcher, "Saturday News of New Books," Chicago *Daily Tribune*, October 30, 1937, p. 14, col. 3; N. L. Rothman, "Albert Halper's Industrial Novel," *The Saturday Review of Literature*, XVII (November 6, 1937), 6; "Hard-Driven Workers in Halper's Novel," Springfield (Massachusetts) Sunday *Union and Republican*, Dec. 26, 1937, p. 7E, col. 8; Louis Kronenberger, "Mail-Order Movie," *The Nation*, CXLV (November 6, 1937), 512; Harry Thornton Moore, "Zola Americana," *The New Republic*, XCIII (December 1, 1937), 111; Harold Strauss, "Mr. Halper Writes of Mail Order Workers," *The New York Times Book Review*, Sunday, November 7, 1937, p. 7; Granville Hicks, "Review and Comment," *New Masses*, XXV (November 23, 1937), 20–21.

Chapter Six

1. Samuel Eliot Morison, *The Oxford History of the American People* (New York, 1965), p. 987.

2. Ernest Hemingway, *A Farewell to Arms* (New York, 1929), p. 196.

3. Arthur S. Link, *American Epoch, A History of the United States Since the 1890's* (in collaboration with William B. Catton) (New York, 1963), p. 474.

4. *Good-bye, Union Square*, p. 211

5. Morison, p. 989.

6. Archibald MacLeish, *The Irresponsibles, A Declaration* (New York, 1940), p. 3.

7. Albert Halper, *Sons of the Fathers* (New York, 1940, unnumbered page "Author's Note." Subsequent references will appear in the text.

8. Harold Strauss, "What Happened to a 'Little Man' in the Last War," *The New York Times Book Review*, Sunday, October 20, 1940, Sec. 6, p. 5; Griffin Barry, "The Other War," *The New Republic*, CIV (January 27, 1941), 123; Barbara Giles, "World War I," *New Masses*, XXXVIII (December 24, 1940), 24–25; James T. Farrell, "Saul Bergman's Sons," *The Saturday Review of Literature*, XXIII (November 2, 1940), 12.

9. When Halper worked for John T. Shayne & Company, now located at 105 North Michigan Avenue, Chicago, it was located on the State Street side of the Palmer House, the third hotel to bear that name and the most famous one. The seven-story building had been designed by John M. Van Osdel and was built in 1875 at a reported cost of thirteen million dollars. It was to have contained "more bricks than any two hotels on the Continent, and more iron than most of them put together." Rudyard Kipling called it a "gilded and mirrored rabbit warren . . . , crammed with people talking about money and spitting about everywhere." The present hotel, designed by Holabird & Roche, was completed during 1925–27; it is twenty-five stories high and contains 2000 rooms. See Harold M. Mayer and Richard C. Wade, *Chicago: Growth of a Metropolis* (Chicago, 1969), pp. 121 and 463.

10. Albert Halper, *The Little People* (New York, 1942), p. 263. Subsequent references will appear in the text.

11. N. L. Rothman, "Halper . . . ," *The Saturday Review of Literature*, XXV (October 17, 1942), 16.

12. Isaac Rosenfeld, "The Power and the Boredom," *The New Republic* CVII (November 23, 1942), 687.

13. "In Brief," *The Nation*, CLV (October 31, 1942), 457.

14. Lillian Gilkes, "Unsung History," *New Masses*, XLV (November 24, 1942), 24–26. Also see Harold Strauss, "At Sutton & Co.," *The New York Times Book Review*, Sunday, October 11, 1942, Sec. 6, p. 8; Strauss had reviewed four of Halper's books and called this one "by long odds his best."

Chapter Seven

1. *Good-bye, Union Square*, pp. 240–41.

2. Albert Halper, *Only an Inch from Glory* (New York, 1943), p. 14. Subsequent references are included in the text.

3. Albert Halper, *The Fourth Horseman of Miami Beach* (New York, 1968), p. 84. Subsequent references are included in the text.

4. Albert Halper, *The Golden Watch* (New York, 1953), pp. 245–46. On the dust jacket of the volume, *The Golden Watch* is designated a novel.

Halper refers to it both as a novel and as a collection of short stories. As in *On the Shore*, the major characters continue throughout the stories; the given names of his fictional "brothers" are the same as those he had used in *Sons of the Fathers* and *On the Shore*. Subsequent references are included in the text.

5. Nelson Algren, "Record of a Sure Hand," *The Saturday Review of Literature*, XXXVI (March 7, 1953), 28.

6. Ibid.

7. *This is Chicago*, p. viii.

8. Albert Halper, *The Chicago Crime Book* (Cleveland, 1967), p. 14.

9. Ibid., p. 384.

10. Ibid., p. 17.

11. Neither of Halper's plays has been published, but details on the performances are available from *Variety*. See the review of *My Aunt Daisy* in *Variety*, CXCV (September 1, 1954), 84; Robert Ellenstein directed; the play ran from August 23rd to the 28th. For *Top Man* see the review in *Variety*, CC (November 23, 1955), 56. The highly competent cast turned in fine performances; the script received praise, although the reviewer says that the "dialog varies from pedestrian to punchy."

12. *Good-bye, Union Square*, p. 7.

13. Ibid., pp. 3–4.

14. Albert Halper, "Chicago Side-Show," (New York, 1932), p. 22. Also see *On the Shore*, p. 239.

Chapter Eight

1. Freeman Champney, "Albert Halper and His Little People," *Antioch Review*, II (December, 1942), 629.

2. Ibid., p. 633.

3. Albert Halper, Letter to Marshall Best, April 20, 1931.

4. *Good-bye, Union Square*, p. 266.

Selected Bibliography

PRIMARY SOURCES

1. Books

Purple Pudding [poetry]. Chicago: privately printed, 1927.

Union Square. New York: The Viking Press, 1933.

On the Shore, Young Writer Remembering Chicago [short stories]. New York: The Viking Press, 1934.

The Foundry. New York: The Viking Press, 1934.

The Chute. New York: The Viking Press, 1937.

Sons of the Fathers. New York: Harper & Brothers, 1940.

The Little People. New York: Harper & Brothers, 1942.

Only an Inch from Glory. New York: Harper & Brothers, 1943.

This Is Chicago: An Anthology. (Edited by Albert Halper) New York: Henry Holt and Company, 1952.

The Golden Watch [short stories with illustrations by Aaron Bohrod]. New York: Henry Holt and Company, 1953.

Atlantic Avenue. New York: Dell Publishing Company, 1956.

The Fourth Horseman of Miami Beach. New York: W. W. Norton & Company, 1966.

The Chicago Crime Book anthology, Ed. Albert Halper. Cleveland: World Publishing Company, 1967.

Good-bye, Union Square: A Writer's Memoir of the Thirties. Chicago: Quadrangle Books, 1970.

2. Magazine Publications

"Whites Writing Up the Blacks," *The Dial*, LXXXVI (January, 1929), 29–30.

"Chicago Mail Clerks," *The Debunker*, IX (February, 1929), 3–11. (Ed. E. Haldeman-Julius, Girard, Kansas).

"On the Shore," *The Dial*, LXXXVI (March, 1929), 225–28.

"Brothers Over a Grave," *The Menorah Journal*, XVI (April, 1929), 365–67. (One of two stories under "Commentaries.")

"Relatives," *The Menorah Journal*, XVI (June, 1929), 557–60.

"Five Men and a Woman," *The Bermondsey Book, A Quarterly Review of Life and Literature*, VI (June, July, August, 1929), 100–108. (Published in London, England.)

"The Goose Dinner," *The Midland*, XV (July–August, 1929), 177–183. (One of two items under "The Sketch Book.")

"Hot Night on the West Side," *The Menorah Journal*, XVII (November, 1929), 186–89. (Second of two items under "Commentaries.")

"The Return," *The Menorah Journal*, XVIII (April, 1930), 364–68. (Second of two items under "Commentaries.")

"Memorial," *The Menorah Journal*, XVIII (May, 1930), 460–65. (Second of two items under "Commentaries.")

"From Down South," *Pagany, A Native Quarterly*, I (Summer, 1930), 34–39.

"The Race," *The Midland*, XVI (July–August, 1930), 169–74. (First of two stories under "The Sketch Book.")

"Two Sisters," *Pagany, A Native Quarterly*, I (October–December, 1930), 78–82.

"Young Writer, Remembering Chicago," *The Menorah Journal*, XIX (November–December, 1930), 142–57.

"The Oldest Brother," *Prairie Schooner*, V (Spring, 1931), 168–71.

"Payday on the Night Shift," *Nativity: An American Quarterly*, I (Spring, 1931), 27–30.

"A Farewell to the Rising Son," *Pagany, A Native Quarterly*, II (April–June, 1931), 1–21; II (July–September, 1931), 94–118; II (October–December), 115–132.

"Looking for a Job," *The Left, A Quarterly Review of Radical and Experimental Art*, I (Summer–Autumn, 1931), 64–65.

"White Laughter," *American Caravan IV* (ed. Alfred Kreymborg, Lewis Mumford, Paul Rosenfeld), New York: The Macaulay Company, 1931, pp. 358–66.

"The Big Order," *Clay, A Literary Notebook*, I (Winter, 1931–1932), 32–36.

"Farm Hand," *The New Republic*, LXX (April 6, 1932), 208–10.

"My Brothers Who Are Honest Men," *The American Mercury*, XXV (April, 1932), 491–98.

"Notes on Jewish–American Fiction," *The Menorah Journal*, XX (April–June, 1932), 61–69.

"Winter in My Heart," *Pagany, A Native Quarterly*, III (April–June, 1932), 106–7.

"Summer Camp," *The American Mercury*, XXVI (May, 1932), 75–83.

"Chicago Side-Show," New York: Modern Editions Press, 1932. Pamphlet Series One, No. 6. Illustrated by Louis Lozowick. "Revised version of "Young Writer, Remembering Chicago."

"A Small West Side Family," *Trend*, I (September, October, November, 1932), 87–89.

"Going to Market," *Harper's Monthly Magazine*, CLXV (October, 1932), 592–97.

"A Herring for My Uncle," *The American Mercury*, XXVII (November, 1932), 364–70.

"My Aunt Daisy," *The American Mercury*, XXVII (December, 1932), 486–96.

"Over the Bridge in the Bronx," *Harper's Monthly Magazine*, CLXVI (February, 1933), 319–26.

"Behind the Scenes of *Union Square*," *Wings*, VII (March, 1933), 5–8.

"The Feud in the Rotunda," *The American Mercury*, XXVIII (March, 1933), 305–12.

"The Doctor," *Pagany, A Native Quarterly*, III (Spring, 1933), 66–69.

"The Penny-Divers," *The North American Review*, CCXXXV (May, 1933), 395–405.

"Winter Evening," *The American Mercury*, XXX (September, 1933) 25–31.

"The United Front of the Jews," *American Spectator*, II (November, 1933), 2–3.

"My Mother's Uncle from Lithuania," *The Sunday Review* of the Brooklyn *Daily Eagle*, Section F, December 10, 1933, pp. 10–13.

"A Morning with the Doc," *New Masses*, XI (May 15, 1934), 14–16.

"Scab!" *The American Mercury*, XXXII (June, 1934), 232–37.

A Letter in "Change the World!," a column conducted by Sender Garlin, (New York) *Daily Worker*, Tuesday, June 26, 1934, p. 5.

"The Plight of the Postal Subs," *New Masses*, XII (July 31, 1934), 18–19.

"Hot Night in Rockford," *Esquire*, II (August, 1934), 66–67, 117.

"Milly," *Redbook Magazine*, LXV (May, 1935), 42–45, 109. (Illustrated by Joseph N. Clement.)

"They Do the Same in England," *Partisan Review*, II (July–August, 1935), 29–36.

"Doctor Winton," *The Atlantic Monthly*, CLVI (December, 1935), 703–11.

"Model Wanted," *Esquire*, V (January, 1936), 41, 182B.

"The Poet," *The Virginia Quarterly Review*, XII (April, 1936), 248–59.

"Ernie and the Barber's Daughter," *Parade*, I (Spring, 1936), 7–8, 39–40.

"Child of Sorrow," review of *Low Company* by Daniel Fuchs, *The New Republic*, XC (February 24, 1937), 89–90.

"My Brother's Confirmation," *Direction*, I (June, 1938), 17–22.

"Prelude," *Harper's Monthly Magazine*, CLXXVII (August, 1938), 302–308.

"A Guy like Dostoevski," *Friday Magazine*, I (March 15, 1940), 9, 17, 21. (Illustrated by Don Freeman.)

"The Adventurer," *Old Line* (University of Maryland), XII (April, 1943), 17–18, 30.

"Crime Wave," *New Masses*, XLVII (June 8, 1943), 18–21.

"Fate, Destiny, or Something," *Collier's*, CXII (July 10, 1943), 14, 61–62. Illustrated by Harry Beckhoff.

"Under Forty: A Symposium on American Literature and the Younger Generation of American Jews," *Contemporary Jewish Record*, VII (February, 1944), 23–25.

"The Prophet of Lake Street," *Collier's*, CXIII (March 11, 1944), 13, 61–64. Illustrated by Harry Beckhoff.

"The Call of the Soil," *Collier's*, CXIII (April 1, 1944), 70–71, 73. Illustrated by Harry Beckhoff.

"My Cousin Louie, The Explorer," *Collier's*, CXIII (April 29, 1944), 20, 64, 66–67. Illustrated by Harry Beckhoff.

"Notes on Novel Writing," *The Writer*, LVII (August, 1944), 227–29.

"The Battle of the Boiled Hams," *The Saturday Evening Post*, CCXVII (September 23, 1944), 18, 56, 59, 61, 63. Illustrated by George L. Connelly.

"A Song Writer in the Family," *The Yale Review*, XXXIII (December, 1944), 258–67.

"Should We Outlaw Anti-Semitism," *New Masses*, LIV (January 30, 1945), 5–7.

"Never Bow Down," *Negro Digest*, III (February, 1945), 61–62.

"The Road Home," *The American Magazine*, CXL (August, 1945), 22–23, 87–88, 91–92. Illustrated by John R. Holmgren.

"Play, Tutti, Play," *The American Magazine*, CXL (December, 1945), 36–37, 136–40. Illustrated by Ben Stahl.

"How to Write Realistic Stories," *The Writer*, LIX (March, 1946), 73–74.

"My Mother's Love Story," *Story*, XXVIII (March–April, 1946), 23–32.

"Old-Timer," *Woman's Day* (November, 1946), 40–41, 78–80, 83–86.

"My Father's Broad Shoulders," *The New Yorker*, XXIII (September 6, 1947), 44–50.

"Miss Leland," *Woman's Day* (April, 1948), 36–37, 107–11.

"The Soldier Who Wanted to See Whitman," *Prairie Schooner*, XXII (Spring, 1948), 82–91.

"The Photograph," *The New Yorker*, XXIV (August 4, 1948), 54–59.

"Money," *The Yale Review*, XXXVIII (March, 1949), 520–29.

"Small Matter," *Senior Scholastic*, LIV (April 6, 1949), 23–24.

"Underwater Heroes," *Saga*, I (November, 1950), 26–29, 85–86.

"The Wallet," *The New Yorker*, XXVI (February 3, 1951), 60–65.

"It's the Giant of America's Heartland," *Holiday*, X (October, 1951), 44–55.

"The Big Slide," *Commentary*, XII (December, 1951), 558–563.

"Dynamic Capital of Conventioneers," *The New York Times Magazine*, June 29, 1952, pp. 9, 36–37.

"Dentist," *Commentary*, XXVIII (November, 1959), 421–28.

SECONDARY SOURCES

Recent scholarship has provided two helpful bibliographies of the 1930's: Jackson R. Bryer's annotated checklist of "The Literature of the Thirties: A Selected Checklist of Criticism," pp. 229–43 in *The Thirties: Fiction, Poetry, Drama* Warren French, ed., Deland, Florida: Everett Edwards, Inc., 1967, 1969; and "Selected Bibliography," in Harvey Swados, ed., *The American Writer and the Great Depression*, Indianapolis: The Bobbs-Merrill Company, Inc., 1966, pp. xxxvii–xli.

AARON, DANIEL. *Writers on the Left, Episodes in American Literary Communism.* New York: Harcourt, Brace & World, Inc., 1961. A thorough study of literary radicalism; the notes are rich in source material and suggestions for further investigation.

_____. "The Thirties—Now and Then," *The American Scholar*, XXXV (Summer, 1966), 490–94. Seeks a broader interpretation of the period that includes the problems of scarity and insecurity as well as unions and strikes.

AMES, RUSSELL. ". . . notes and sketches relevant . . . ," *The Carleton Miscellany*, VI (Winter, 1965), 12–18. A personal memoir that recalls Halper's writings in the context of the 1930's.

APPEL, BENJAMIN. "My image of the 1930's . . . ," *The Carleton Miscellany*, VI (Winter, 1956), 19 ff. Recollections of a period when writers, including Halper, sought to relate man to the outer world, not simply to the inner self.

————. "Albert's Halper's New Approach," *The Saturday Review of Literature*, XXVI (October 9, 1943), 18. Compares *Only an Inch from Glory* to Halper's writings of the 1930's.

BERG, LOUIS. "Personal Memoir," *Commentary*, LI (April, 1971), 98–102. In reviewing *Good-bye, Union Square*, Berg gives some of his own memories of Union Square.

CHAMPNEY, FREEMAN. "Albert Halper and His Little People," *Antioch Review*, II (December, 1942), 628–34. Sympathetic analysis of Halper's early work that interprets it as providing a unique picture of urban America.

COWLEY, MALCOLM. "The 1930's Were an Age of Faith," *The New York Times Book Review*, December 13, 1964, pp. 4–5, 14–16. Important reassessment of the decade as an age of hard to define faith.

EISINGER, CHESTER E. "Character and Self in Fiction on the Left," *Proletarian Writers of the Thirties*, David Madden, ed. Carbondale and Edwardsville: Southern Illinois University Press, 1968, pp. 162–65. Berates Halper for not dealing adequately with the artistic problem of man's concern for self.

GELFANT, BLANCHE HOUSMAN. *The American City Novel*. Norman: University of Oklahoma Press, 1954. Brief reference to *Only an Inch from Glory* as exhibiting the theme of the country youth in the city; no mention of Halper's other city novels.

GILBERT, JAMES BURKHART. *Writers and Partisans, A History of Literary Radicalism in America*. New York: John Wiley and Sons, Inc., 1968. A history of the *Partisan Review* in particular and of avant-garde literature in general; the "Bibliographic Essay," pp. 283–91, includes a variety of titles.

HART, JOHN E. "Albert Halper's World of the Thirties," *Twentieth Century Literature*, IX (January, 1964), 185–95. Analyzes the form and themes of *Union Square*, *The Foundry*, and *The Chute*.

HATCHER, HARLAN. *Creating the Modern American Novel*. New York: Farrar & Rinehart, 1935. Brief mention of Halper's early novels as part of the "proletarian" scene.

HERRICK, ROBERT. "Writers in the Jungle," *The New Republic*, LXXX (October 17, 1934), 259–61. Discusses the "social question" as a recurring theme in literature; brief mention of *The Foundry*.

KLEIN, MARCUS. "The Roots of Radicals: Experience in the Thirties," *Proletarian Writers of the Thirties*, David Madden, ed. Carbondale and Edwardsville: Southern Illinois University Press, 1968, pp. 145–48. In

Union Square the irony prevents the characters from realizing the "demands of reality."

LUCCOCK, HALFORD E. *American Mirror—Social, Ethical and Religious Aspects of American Literature 1930–1940.* New York: The Macmillan Company, 1940. Sympathetic and thoughtful analysis of Halper's writing as social and ethical statement.

STOTT, WILLIAM. *Documentary Expression and Thirties America.* New York: Oxford University Press, 1973. A perceptive treatment of a new direction in art, politics, and society; the bibliographic essay, pp. 348–53, is evaluative and informative. The following bibliography for Halper is selective. With only few exceptions, items which have already appeared as references in separate chapters are not listed here.

TERKEL, STUDS. "The Hoods Among Us," *Book World* of the Chicago *Tribune*, December 3, 1967, p. 22. Review of *The Chicago Crime Book* that discusses newspaper writers and suggests choices that Halper failed to include.

WITHAM, W. TASKER. *The Adolescent in the American Novel 1920–1960.* New York: Frederick Ungar Publishing Company, 1964. Brief mention of *The Chute* and *The Golden Watch* as examples of the adolescent in a city environment.

Index